THE ESSENTIAL
MYSTICS,
POETS,
SAINTS,
AND SAGES

THE
ESSENTIAL
MYSTICS,
P⊙ETS,
SAINTS,
AND SAGES

A Wisdom Treasury

Edited and with an introduction by
Richard J. Hooper, M. Div.

HAMPTON ROADS

This edition first published as *Hymns to the Beloved* in 2010
by Sanctuary Publications

Cover design by Nita Ybarra
Interior designed by Kathryn Sky-Peck

Hampton Roads Publishing Company, Inc.
Charlottesville, VA 22906
Distributed by Red Wheel/Weiser, LLC
www.redwheelweiser.com

Sign up for our newsletter and special offers by going to www.redwheelweiser.com/newsletter

ISBN: 978-1-57174-693-1

Library of Congress Cataloging-in-Publication Data available upon request

Printed on acid-free paper in the United States of America

VG

10 9 8 7 6 5 4 3 2 1

To the One who is in all.

CONTENTS

POETS/MYSTICS INSIDE

Christian Mystics

Angelus Silesius
 1624-1677, Germany

Beatrice of Nazareth
 1200-1268, Flanders

Catherine of Siena
 1347-1380, Italy

Clare of Assisi
 1194-1253, Italy

Dame Catherine Gascoigne
 1600-1676, England

Dante Alighieri
 1265-1321, Italy

Dionysius the Areopagite
 5th cent., Greece

Edith Stein
 1891-1942, Germany

Emily Brontë
 1818-1848, England

Francis of Assisi
 1182-1226, Italy

Hadewijch
 13th Cent., Holland

Hildegard of Bingen
 1098-1179, Germany

Jacopone da Todi
 1236-1306, Italy

Jesus
 0000-0033, Israel

John of the Cross
 1542-1591, Spain

Marguerite Porete
 14th cent., France

Meister Eckhart
 1260-1328, Germany

Mechthild of Magdeburg
 1207-1282, Germany

Mother Julian of Norwich
 1342-1416, England

Paul Tillich
 1886-1965, Germany

Pierre Teilhard De Chardin
 1881-1955, France

Ramon Llull
 1232-1315, Spain

Reinhold Niebuhr
1892-1971, Germany

Symeon the New Theologian
949-1022, Turkey

Teresa of Avila
1515-1582, Spain

Thérèse of Lisieux
1873-1897, France

Thomas a' Kempis
1380-1471, Germany

Thomas Merton
1915-1968, USA

Thomas Traherne
1637?-1674, England

Vladimir Solovyov
1853-1900, Russia

Vittoria de Colonna
1490-1547, Italy

Plus readings from the Canonical
and Gnostic Gospels and other
early Christian texts

Sufi Mystics

Abu-Said Abil-Kheir
967-1049, Turkmenistan

Abu'I Husyn-Nuri
Unknown

Abdul-Qader Bedil
1642-1720, Persia (Iran)

Al Ghazzoli
Unknown

Al-Qozat Hamadani
Unknown

Attar
1142-1220, Persia

Ayn al Qozat
1098-1131, Persia

Baba Kuhi Shiraz
980?-1050, Persia

Binavi Badakhshani
13th cent., Afghanistan

Bulleh Shah
1680-1758, India

Farid ud-Din Attar, Iraqi
13th cent., Persia

Francis Brabzaon
1907-1984, Australia

Hafiz
    1320-1390, Persia

Hakim Abu–al-Majd
    1080-1141, Afghanistan

Hakim Sani
    12th cent., Afghanistan

Hazrat Inayat Khan
    1887-1927, India

Imadeddin Nasimi
    1369-1418, Azerbaijan

Javad Nurbakhsh
    1926-2008, Iran

Jelaluddin Rumi
    1207-1273, Persia

Kabir
    1440-1518, India

Khwaja Abdullah Ansari
    1006-1088, Afghanistan

Meher Baba
    1894-1964, India

Mansur al-Hallaj Al Hallaj
    858-922, Persia

Moulana Shah Maghsoud
    1914-1980, Iran

Muhyaddin ibi' Aribi
    1165-1240, Spain

Niffari
    10th cent., Egypt

Niyazi Misri
    1616-1694, Turkey

Qushayri
    11th cent., Persia

Rabi'a Al-Adawiyya
    717-801, Iraq

Rahman Baba
    1652-1701, Afghanistan

Sarmad
    17th cent.

Shah Abdul Latif Bhitai
    1689-1752, Pakistan

Sharib Nawaz
    1141-1230, Pakistan

Sultan Bahu
    1625-1691, Persia

Sultan Valad
    1240-1312, Turkey

Vedanta (Hindu) Mystics

Akka Mahadevi
12th cent., India

Basava
1134-1196, India

Bhaga Namdev
1270-1350, India

Dariya
1674-1780, India

Darshan Sing
1921-1989, India

Derva Dasimayya
10th Cent., India

Eknath Easwaran
1910-1999, India

Guru Nanak
1469-1539, India

Janabai
13th cent., India

Janadev
1275-1296, India

Kalidasa
4th or 5th cent., India

Mahatma Gandhi
1869-1948, India

Mirabai
1498-1550, India

Osho (Bhagavan Sree Rajneesh)
1931-1990, India

Patanjali
2nd cent. B.C.E., India

Paramahansa Yogananda
1893-1952, India

Rabindranath Tagore
1861-1941, India

Ram Dass (Richard Alpert)
1931 - , U.S.

Ramana Maharshi
1879-1950, India

Ramprasad Sen
1723-1775, India

Sathya Sai Baba
1926-2011, India

Shankara
788-820, India

Sri Anandamayi Ma
1896-1982, India

Sri Aurobindo
1872-1950, India

Sri Chinmoy
1931-2007, India

Sri Ramakrishna
1836-1886, India

Sri Sukhabodhananda
Unknown

Swami Akhilananda
1926-1962, India/US

Swami Sai Premananda
1972-2011, West Indies

Swami Muktananda
1908-1982, India

Swami Rama
1925-1996, India

Swami Satchidananda
1914-2002, India

Swami Sivananda
1887-1963, India

Swami Vielammada
Unknown

Swami Vivekananda
1863-1972, India

Tiruvalluvar
1st cent. B.C.E., India

Vidyapati
1352-1448, India

Yogi Bhajan
1929-2004, India

Yagaswami
1872-1964, Sri Lanka

Plus readings from the Vedas,
Upanishads, and Bhagavad
Gita, Srimad Bhagavatam

Buddhist Mystics

Alan Watts
1915-1973, Britain

Bodhidharma
6th cent., China

Buddha
500 B.C.E., India

Chao-Chou Ts'ung-shen
778-897, China

Chiao Jan
8th cent., China

Ching-Yuan
660-740, China

Chiyono Hasegawa
1896-2011

Chogyam Trungpa Rimpoche
1939-1987, Tibet

Dogen
1200-1253, Japan

Feng Kan
8th cent., China

Great Kamo Priestess Senshi
964-1035, Japan

Han-Shan
730-850, China

Hsuan Chuen
Unknown, China

Hsu Yun
1840-1959, China

Hakuen
12th cent., Japan

Kelsan Gyatso
1708-1757, Tibet

Layman Seiken
11th cent., Japan

Ma-tsu Tao i
709-788, Japan

Matsuo Basho
1644-1694, Japan

Milarepa
1052-1135, Tibet

Myochi Roko Sherry Chayat
1940- , USA

Nagarjuna
150-250?, India

Naropa
1016-1100, Tibet

Padmasambhava
8th cent., Tibet

P'ang Yun
740?-808, China

Pema Chödrön
Contemporary, Nova Scotia

Saraha
    1st or 2nd cent., India
Sakyong Mishram Rimpoche
    1962- , India
Saryajnamita
    8th cent., Kashmir
Sengai Bibon
    1750-1837, Japan
Seng Ts'an
    D. 606, Japan
Sen-no-Rikyu
    1522-1591, Japan
Shabkar
    1781-1837, Tibet
Shih-shu
    17th cent., China
Sumangalamata
    6th cent. B.C.E., India
Sun Bu-er
    Unknown
Su yun
    Unknown
Ta'o Chien
    Unknown
Tenzin Gyatso,
    the 14th Dalai Lama
    1935- , Tibet
Thich Nhat Hanh,
    1929- , Vietnam

Tu Fu
    Unknown
Van Hanh
    11th cent., Vietnam
Wang Wei
    699?-761, China
Wu Men
    1183-1260, China
Yasutani Roshi
    1885-1973, Japan
Yeshe Tsogyel
    8th cent., Tibet
Yoka Genkaku
    665-713, China
Yuquan Shenxiu
    670-762, China
Yung Chia
    7th cent., China
Yun-men
    864-949, China
Zengetsu
    Tang Dynasty, China

Plus readings from the Pali
    Canon, *The Dhammapada, The
    Diamond Sutra,* and various other
    sutras

Taoist Mystics

Chuang Tzu
369-286 B.C.E., China

Chi K'ang
224-263, China

Chio Jan
730-799, China

Han-shan
730-850, China

Huai-nan-Tzu
2nd cent. B.C.E.

Lao Tzu c.
600-300 B.C.E., China

Li Po
701-762, China

Loy Ching-Yuen
1873-1960

Sun-Bu-er
1119-1182, China

T'ao Ch-ien
365-427, China

Tu Fu
712-770, China

Wong We Sheh-Tou
Unknown

Yan Mei
1716-1798, China

Yoka Genkaku
665-713, China

Yuan Lu Tung-Pin
B. 726 E.E., China

Jewish Mystics

Abraham ben Samuel Abulafia
1240-1295?, Spain

Abraham Joshua Heschel
1907-1972, Poland

Eleazar ben Kallir
6th century, Israel

Isaac of Acco
13th or 14th cent., Israel

Judah Halevi
1075-1141, Spain

Levi Yitzchak
1740-1810, Poland

Maggid of Merzeritch
1710?-1772, Poland

Moses ben Jacob Cordovero
1522-1570, Spain

Moses De Leon
(Moses ben Shem Tov)
1245?-1270, Spain

Nachmanides
1194-?, Spain

Nachman of Bratzlav
1772-1810, Ukraine

Sarmad
?-1659, Persia

Solomon 'ibn-Gabirol
1021?-1058, Spain

Yanni
6th cent., Israel

Plus readings from the Bible and
the Zohar

Nonsectarian

Albert Einstein
1879-1955, Germany

Alice Bailey
1880-1949, England

Andrew Cohen
1955- , USA

Aldous Huxley
1894-1963, England

David Hawkins
1913-2012, USA

Czeslaw Milosz
1911-2004, Poland

Eckhart Tolle
1948- , Germany

Eileen Caddy
1917-2006, Egypt

Gabriela Mistral
1889-1957, Chile

Henry David Thoreau
1817-1862, USA

J. Krishnamurti
1895-1986, India

Juan Ramon Jimenez
1881-1958, Andalusia

Kahlil Gibran
1883-1931, Lebanon

Olga Ramussen
Unknown

Plato
c. 428 B.C.E., Greece

Plotinus
205-270, Egypt

Rainer Maria Rilke
1875-1926, Austria

Theodore Roethke
1908-1963, USA

Thomas Treherne
1630-1674, England

William Blake
1757-1827, England

THE OPENING VERSES

Don't believe something just because somebody tells you it's true, or you read it in scriptures. Don't even believe what your teachers tell you unless your own reason and experience confirms what they say.

THE BUDDHA

Don't depend on or believe any particular creed exclusively, so that you reject all other creeds. If you do so you will lose the benefit of a wider knowledge and will not be able to see the real truth. Recognize the real truth of the matter. God, the omnipresent and omnipotent, is not limited by any one creed.

IBN AL-ARIBI, SUFI

Different religions teach different paths to the one Source. But teachings are not God, and all paths have their own failings.

SRI RAMAKRISHNA, VEDANTA (HINDU)

Truth is truth no matter what religion teaches it.
All paths lead to the same Source, and the differences are only semantic.

MEHER BABA, SUFI

The only temple that matters can be found within yourself.

TENZIN GYATSO, HIS HOLINESS, THE FOURTEENTH DALAI LAMA

I consider myself a Hindu, Christian, Muslim,
Jew, Buddhist and Confucian.

MAHATMA GANDHI

If you wish to understand the teachings in this book,
you must be humble and open.
Love and faith will let you rise above reason.

MARGUERITE PORETE, *THE MIRROR OF SIMPLE SOULS*

INTRODUCTION

THE PERENNIAL PHILOSOPHY

Mysticism is not merely an adjunct to a religion, nor is it a religion unto itself. It is, rather, what Aldous Huxley called The Perennial Philosophy, the viewpoint and doorway that leads to the path that ends in *union* with Ultimate Reality, or the Ground of All Being. Mysticism is the attempt to gain *direct* experience of Ultimate Reality through achieving a state of consciousness that Eastern religions call "Enlightenment."

Most mystical traditions evolved out of formal religions, or at least within a specific religious milieu. There were, of course, the ancient Greek mystic philosophers like Pythagoras, Plato, Democritus, and Plotinus. Even the Jewish philosopher Philo of Alexandria held ideas similar to those found in Hinduism and Buddhism.

Still, these men were philosophers, and philosophers approach the problem of existence from the outside, while mystics turn within themselves for answers. Philosophers can theorize that "All is One," yet they cannot experience the Reality itself unless they follow the path of the mystics.

The word "mysticism" means different things to different people, but in this book it will refer only to the inner-directed effort of the individual to realize complete union with the Absolute—to realize our already existing Oneness with all things, or Ultimate Reality.

This Ultimate Reality, the mystics tell us, is both immanent—pervading all that exists in the phenomenal world—and transcendent—pervading all universes and whatever lies beyond all universes. According to most mystics, this "God," if you will, is entirely impersonal and may or may not even be aware of Itself. The "Ground of Being" may or may not be Self-conscious.

The cosmology associated with mysticism is monistic rather than dualistic. In mysticism, there is only one Reality in the universe, not two. "God" alone exists. But "God" is not simply equal to all that exists (pantheism), but is also beyond all things (pan-en-theism). The Absolute contains all things, but it is simultaneously beyond all things. It is immanent and transcendent simultaneously.

Mysticism is the realm of higher consciousness and altered reality. The All may be known only when the individual mystic—the ego-self—completely disappears, so all that remains is the One.

Anyone who has lived long enough on this planet to observe history and human nature can easily be frustrated that religion—indeed, all human endeavors—has not succeeded in making the world what it could be. We can have sympathy for the mindset of the biblical author of Ecclesiastes who declared twenty-three hundred years ago that all human endeavors are, in the end, vanity.

Were it not for this recognition, this disappointment with the world, mysticism might never have arisen in any religion—for it is this very frustration that leads some to conclude that if we cannot change the world, we *can* change our perception of it.

Both the Buddha and Jesus understood the human condition and the nature of the illusory world. While they counseled their followers to heal the sick and feed the hungry, they also told them that they should not expect to find happiness in this illusory realm. Instead of trying to change the world, they taught, we should turn inward in an effort to change ourselves.

Ironically, it is only when interior illumination is finally attained that one suddenly perceives the world in an entirely different way—as transformed! The Kingdom of God, Jesus said, has always been here—both within us and all around us—we simply haven't been capable of seeing it. And it is only when our eyes are completely open that we become fully capable of having compassion for all living beings.

One thing we may perceive in growing older is that good and evil are inextricably mixed. Knowledge, happiness, success, and perfection turn out to be idealized illusions. The Buddha was correct: suffering is the human condition, or at least one aspect of it. And the Buddha would also agree that traditional—religious, political, or social—approaches to ending suffering will always fail.

In the end we cannot change how the universe works. If we still want to be happy in life, we are left with only one option: change ourselves; that is, change our own perception of the world. Mysticism holds out the possibility that with enough insight into the nature of Reality, we might just discover that all things are as they should be—the way they are meant to be, if not the way we would prefer them to be.

The Kingdom of God is not something outside of ourselves; it has been within us all along. The Kingdom of God is not some perfect utopia yet to come. It is here, now; it is within us and all around us. But we can only *enter* it when we develop mystical eyes to see and ears to hear. The Kingdom becomes evident the moment our perception of Reality changes.

In my experience the Kingdom is real, for I've been there and seen it for myself. Many years ago I had an abrupt and totally unexpected change of consciousness that lasted a full week, and it was the result of an act of utter surrender to divine will. At the time my personality was such that it didn't take a lot to push my buttons. I was often defensive, grumpy, and judgmental. But in this altered state of consciousness, nothing—literally nothing—could upset me. Not only did I not express anger, there was no anger to express. Anger itself did not exist in my consciousness. I had but a single attitude and a single response to everything that happened around me: unconditional love and unbearable compassion for every living being.

This consciousness ended abruptly after seven straight days, and I understood then, as I understand now, that I had experienced an instance of cosmic grace. Grace allowed me to experience firsthand what life would be like all the time if only my consciousness were permanently altered. This consciousness is the pearl of great price to which Jesus referred. For Hindus and Buddhists, it is the jewel within the lotus. It seems to me that the personal quest for such a treasure is the most worthy goal of any life.

I was a religious person at the time this event took place. Quite possibly I would not have had this experience had it not been for my religious faith. But the experience itself transcended all religious doctrines and dogmas.

We hardly need to be reminded about the limitations of religion. Throughout history religions have caused wars, fostered terrorism in small and great ways, and very often killed their own prophets and mystics.

Marguerite Porete, quoted earlier, was a fourteenth century Roman Catholic nun. She was also a mystic, and that led to her being burned at the stake by the Inquisition in 1310 C.E. The evidence against her was her own book, *The Mirror of Simple Souls,* in which she was audacious enough to suggest a non-dualistic universe, and to describe how the soul could unite with the Divine.

But without religion, Jesus, the Buddha, Saint Francis, and Mahatma Gandhi might never have graced this earth. Religions have always been the ferries that deliver to our shores the profound insights of humanity's spiritual giants.

Since the mystical experience transcends religious dogma and allows one to have direct insight into the nature of Reality, we should not be surprised that the essential understanding of all true mystics is, in all the most important ways, identical. And since these men and women came from different religions and cultures, neither should we be surprised that they used, and continue to use, different religious metaphors to describe their understanding of Ultimate Reality.

Thus, the validity of the mystical experience is confirmed not by differences, but by what mystics hold in common. William James, in his *Varieties of Religious Experience*, states that overcoming "... all the usual barriers between the individual and the Absolute is the great mystic achievement. In mystic states we become one with the Absolute and we become aware of our oneness. This is the everlasting and triumphant mystic tradition, hardly altered by differences of clime and creed.

"In Hinduism, in Neo-Platonism, in Sufism, in Christian mysticism, all these men and women overcame all the usual barriers between the individual and the Absolute. Nothing less than the unification of the individual with its Source of Being was, for them, a passionate necessity."

Many students of religious texts assume that those mystics in Hindu, Sufi, Christian, (and even Jewish) traditions who use the metaphor of the "lover" and "the Beloved" were, by definition, dualists. After all, the metaphor of lover and Beloved seems to suggest both a subject and an object. But this is a wrong assumption. I believe that the mystics' own words in this book will irrefutably demonstrate that they were all monists, not dualists—for the realization of Oneness is the very nature of the mystical experience.

There are those who would disagree, but I believe that the various philosophical differences between one mystical tradition and another are ultimately irrelevant and unimportant. All *true* mystics seek union with the All. They also recognize that physical phenomena are, essentially, illusory. All mystics also recognize that the only way to reach their goal of union with the One is through the sacrifice of their own ego-identity.

It should not matter that different mystics use different metaphors and cultural/religious language to describe their interpretation of the Absolute. No matter what name mystics choose to use when speaking of Ultimate Reality, be it "God," "Brahman," "Buddha-nature," "Nirvana," or the "Beloved," they are all talking about the same Reality.

That some mystics, whether Jews, Christians, Sufi Muslims, or Hindus, use "God language," while Buddhists and Taoists do not, is really irrelevant. When we are speaking about the abstract and impersonal aspect of the Supreme, we call it the Absolute. When we want to emphasize the Absolute as a self-aware, self-blissful being, we might use the word "God."

That which is Real is beyond all names and all conceptions of personality and impersonality. The attempt to give *That-Which-Is* any name at all reflects the inadequacy of all terms and definitions. If we use the word "God," while the implication seems personal, it refers to the basis of all that exists, and is the goal of all. The "personality" of the Godhead is nothing more than a metaphor and a symbol, and if we ignore its symbolic nature we miss the truth.

Though religions themselves seem divisive, the opposite is the case for religious mystics. No matter what religious tradition the mystic comes from, he or she speaks not of division, but of unity. Such spiritual giants have unshakable faith in the supremacy of Spirit, together with invincible optimism, ethical universalism, and religious toleration.

Cultural and religious influences, however, are not the only reason some mystics use metaphorical, dualistic language. The case of Marguerite Porete is but one example of how dangerous it is to be a mystic within dualistic religious traditions. For this reason, mystics within Jewish, Christian, and Islamic traditions have sometimes found it necessary to use coded language to describe their experiences. In theory, this (dualistic) coded language serves as protection against heresy hunters. But using the metaphor of the lover and the Beloved to describe one's relationship to the All doesn't always work.

The Sufi Muslim mystic Abu Yazid, who died in 875 C.E., was able to get away with writing about the extinction of the empirical self as the mystic melts into God. He further dared to write that one achieves this union with God, not necessarily by prostrating oneself and praying to Allah, but by self-control—ascetic and contemplative practices which ultimately lead to a state wherein all consciousness of one's own individuality as separate from God is lost. Less than a century later, however, another great Sufi mystic, Al Hallaj, was both crucified *and* beheaded for daring to proclaim his identity with Allah.

14

THE LOVER AND THE BELOVED

The metaphor of the Lover-Beloved parallels the Hindu concept of Atman-Brahman. Atman, or Self—the localized divinity within—*is* Brahman, or God. When the "Lover" (the individuated divine Self) melts into the Beloved, only the Beloved remains. Once Atman is fully recognized as identical to Brahman, only Brahman remains. Duality, for mystics, is an illusion.

Christian and Sufi mystics use "God language" because they are comfortable with it, and while Hindus refer to Brahman as "God," Brahman is not a deity in any true sense of the word. Brahman is the wholly impersonal Absolute. Christian and Sufi mystics use the term "God" in the same way.

While the Christian or Sufi mystic's ultimate goal is no different from that of a Buddhist or Hindu, there are differences between their metaphors, emphasis, philosophy, and practice. The writings of Christian and Sufi mystics—and in many cases, Hindus as well—are often ecstatic in nature. The human traits of passion and emotion are common to Christian, Sufi, Jewish, and Hindu mystical literature, whereas they seem less present in Taoism and Buddhism.

There are several reasons for these differences, and they are all essentially philosophical. Hindus may "worship" different gods like

Shiva or Vishnu or Ishvara, but their expression of devotion is not really polytheistic. The Godhead of Brahman describes Brahman's function: Brahma represents the Creator of life, Vishnu the Sustainer, and Shiva the Destroyer.

Tibetan Buddhism may be similarly misunderstood given its devotion to a pantheon of deities. This may seem paradoxical since Buddhists do not believe in a theistic God.

But when mystic ecstasy and the personified metaphor of "God" or the "Beloved" is missing, spiritual poetry is often missing as well. Hymns and prayers to the Beloved seem to be highly emotional. Buddhism discourages emotions in favor of achieving equanimity of mind, so it has no foundation for ecstatic poetry. Likewise, Buddhism rejects the metaphor of the Beloved—believing (falsely, in my opinion) it to be a theistic term.

Chan Buddhists of China and Zen Buddhists of Japan, on the other hand, are masters of haiku-like, intentionally cryptic, poetry written in such a way as to force the reader to use the intuitive, not the discursive, mind. Since ancient Chinese Taoism had a major influence on Buddhism when it first came to China, there are parallels between Taoist and Zen poetry.

Buddhists also refer to the Absolute as the "Void" or *Sunyata*. By definition, Buddhism is—at least metaphorically—nihilistic, and nihilism is hardly an incubator for poetry. Still, Chan and Zen Buddhist literature is often poetic. Consider the words of the Third Chinese patriarch of Zen:

The Great Way (Tao) is not difficult for those who have no preferences. When love and hate are both absent, everything becomes clear and undisguised. Make the slightest distinction, however, and heaven and earth are set infinitely apart.

This particular Buddhist text is quite beautiful prose, partly due to the particular translation, and partly due to the influence of Taoism. Taoist poetry also lacks ecstatic language, but the verses attributed to Lao Tzu in *The Tao Te Ching*, as well as those written by other early Taoists, are often highly poetic. If these poems are not ecstatic in nature, they still give us a sense of the sublime.

THE NATURE OF PERCEPTION

Although Buddhists are a-theistic, the historical Buddha never specifically denied the existence of "God." He simply had no use for ontological debate on the subject. He pointed out that philosophizing about the nature of Reality was pointless; it did not relieve suffering. For the Buddha, the most important goal was to discover the nature of the mind that *perceives* Reality!

Just as Jesus used parables to encourage his listeners to access their intuitive minds, the Buddha did not tell his disciples what the true nature of *mind* is. Instead, he encouraged them to find out for themselves. Using a dialectic form of teaching, the Buddha rejected every answer about the nature of mind that came from intellectual reasoning rather than from direct insight.

In the Zen Buddhist tradition, Zen masters give novice monks a riddle, or koan, to solve. The riddle, however, is intentionally unsolvable. The monk doesn't fully comprehend this at first, so he makes an all-out effort to *solve* the riddle using the reasoning process of his mind. Every time the monk thinks he has the right answer, he tells the Zen master. But instead of praise he receives a whack from the Zen master's bamboo cane.

By using this method of teaching, the Zen master is trying to push the monk's discursive mind to the breaking point. If a monk is ultimately successful, it is only because his thinking mind finally short-circuits. The moment the mind exhausts itself and shuts down—wham! Satori!

One day after long years of practice on the part of the monk, the Zen master asks for the solution to the riddle yet again. While this time the monk gives an answer that would make little sense to you or me, the Zen master perceives it differently. Instead of smacking the monk with his cane, he just smiles—knowing that the monk has finally attained illumination.

Years ago it occurred to me that I had no objective means of knowing whether what I perceived as "objective" reality was, in fact, objectively real. The philosophy of solipsism holds that no reality exists outside the individual mind. While I was not ready to go that far, I did understand that I could not confirm the existence—or the nonexistence—of objective reality because supposedly objective information was still being processed through my subjective mind.

Such philosophizing tends to annoy people. Were I to state these sentiments to someone, he or she might stomp on my foot, and ask: "Oh, yeah? Is that pain objectively real or not?" I would only annoy them further—and gain a second crippled foot—by stating that there was still no way of knowing. The pain, after all, was subjective. In our normal, or *default* consciousness there is simply no way to confirm or deny objective reality.

Perception is the essence of mysticism, and that raises an important consideration. If we attain Enlightenment, the enlightened experience itself is, quite literally, subjective. This may account for the different ways mystics describe Ultimate Reality.

It also appears that there are different stages and levels of Enlightenment. The Hindu's experience of Samadhi is described as a state of bliss, and doesn't sound quite like the Zen experience of Satori. And Zen Satori doesn't sound quite like the final Buddhist experience of Nirvana.

Though Hindu, Christian, and Sufi mystics often describe their experience of Ultimate Reality in ecstatic terms, one can also find in their literature the warning not to remain in this state. Buddhists take this for granted. Ecstasy, bliss, is apparently not the highest state of awareness.

If Buddhists pay little attention to states of ecstasy in their literature, it is probably not because they don't experience them, but because ecstasy represents just one more level of consciousness where one can get stuck. After all, ecstatic states of consciousness can be achieved by using psychedelic drugs, but the drug experience is not Enlightenment.

Taoist mystical expression is different yet again. The ancient Taoists wrote about achieving *harmony* with Tao, the way things are; to go with the flow, not against it. As a consequence, much of Taoist literature, like much of Chan Buddhist literature, is based on becoming completely transparent to the natural order of things. To disappear into Tao, to become nobody, is stressed in all mystical systems, but it is emphasized most often in Taoist poetry.

Jewish mysticism is unique from all other systems. It cannot be properly understood apart from Judaism itself. While the essence of Hindu, Sufi, and Buddhist thought has remained essentially the same over the past two thousand years, Jewish mysticism has taken great leaps in one direction or another during the same period of time.

The earliest period of Jewish mysticism had much in common with Gnostic philosophy. The ecstatic ascent of the soul to the highest realm can be found in both systems during the first millennium of the Common Era. The latest incarnation of Jewish mysticism is Hassidism, and it contains few of the elements found in early Jewish mysticism. Since Jewish mysticism is highly esoteric, it is not easily understood by those who stand outside the tradition of Judaism.

Jewish mysticism today is represented symbolically by the *Sephiroth*, the inverted Tree of Life—interconnected circles, with names representing levels of consciousness. Each circle represents a focus for attention, and a symbolic method for making spiritual progress. The anonymous author of the book, *Toward the One*, states:

> From *Malkuth* (Kingdom), the lowest level of awareness . . .
>
> One can rise to *Yesod* (foundation) by thinking of the body as part of the fabric of the planet; rise to *Hod* (majesty) by giving up the image of the self, and reach *Netsach* (perpetuality) by abandoning the mind to its own devices; and reach *Tiphereth* (adornment-mercy) by emotional sublimation, giving up the notion of the self; and reach *Geburah* (strength-judgment-power) by abandoning the notion of contingency or entities; and reach *Chesed* (loving kindness) by overcoming karma by love; and reach *Binah* (heart/left hemisphere of the brain) by giving up acuity; and reach *Dhokma* (the mystical state in which all ten *Sephirot* are united as one) by realizing that the causes of all events are intended to conceal Reality; and reaches *Kether* (the crown—the most hidden of all hidden things) in the consternation of intelligence. In the noughting of unity one reaches *Ain Soph* (infinity or nameless being) by ceasing to be.

Though bridges between mystical systems can be hard to build, the similarities of the mystical experience far outweigh the dissimilarities. All mystics describe the experience of Enlightenment as a sense of complete loss of one's ego-identity, and a complete absorption into the *One*—no matter what words are used to describe the One. The goal of all mysticism is the same.

One Buddhist scholar who tried to bridge the gap between Christian mysticism and Zen Buddhism was D.T. Susuki. He understood that the common goal of both systems was to discover reality beyond form. In his book, *Mysticism: Christian and Buddhist,* he makes many parallels between the teachings of Meister Eckhart and Zen Buddhism.

Meister Eckhart, himself a Christian monk, summed up his philosophy as follows:

> When I preach, I usually speak of detachment and say that a man
> should be empty of self and all things; and secondly, that he should
> be reconstructed in the simple good that God is; and thirdly, that
> he should consider the great aristocracy which God has set up in
> the soul, such that by means of it man may wonderfully attain to
> God; and fourthly, of the purity of the divine nature.

One could replace the word *God* with *Buddha-nature* in Eckhart's statement, and it wouldn't really much matter. These words are only human constructs that are ultimately empty of meaning. Because the mystical experience itself is ineffable, religions and mystical traditions are limited in being able to describe the nature of the Absolute in words. To some extent, they are like the fabled blind men describing an elephant by touching only one part of it. Mystical language is *always* metaphorical.

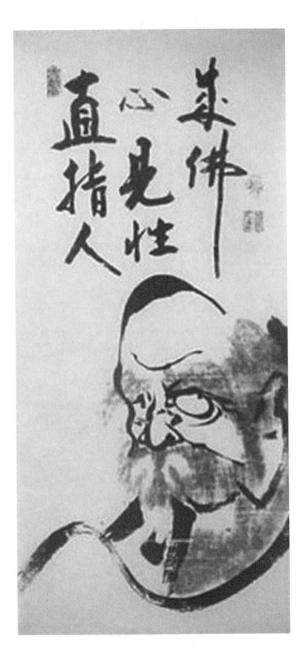

NAMING THE UNNAMEABLE ONE

That-Which-Is, is beyond name and beyond form. It can be given names, or no name at all. All names for the ultimate ground of being can never be more than metaphors: *Ultimate Reality*, the *Absolute*, *Universal Mind*, *Buddha-nature*, *Brahman*, the *All*, *Ain Soph*, the *Great Spirit*, *Tao*, or the *Force*. In the end, Lao Tzu, in *The Tao Te Ching* simply calls it Tao:

> The Tao that can be named, is not the everlasting Tao.
> Names can be given to it, but not the timeless name.
> As that which stands behind creation, it is nameless.
>
> As that which gives birth to creation, it is nameable. Because it is Reality Unseen, we should seek its hidden essence. Because it is Reality Seen, we should seek to understand its manifest nature.
>
> Both aspects flow from the same Source. Both are called mysteries, and the mystery of mystery is the gateway to the Essence that lies behind mysteries.

On one occasion when I was present at a conference of progressive Christian academics, the well known professor of New Testament studies, Marcus Borg (an out-of-the-closet mystic), was pressed by a skeptical peer (an atheist) to define what he meant when he used the word "God." After a little hedging, Borg responded with an invented word: "Is-ness."

This answer only infuriated his inquisitor, who demanded that Borg define "Is-ness." I think the audience knew that Professor Borg was not going to be able to get through to an atheistic academic who was firmly rooted in the reasoning mind.

As for "Is-ness," Buddhists often use a similar word: "Suchness" (*Thathagatta*) to name the Absolute. Two thousand years ago, the Buddhist sage Ashvaghosha wrote: "Suchness is neither that which is existence nor that which is nonexistence, nor that which is at once existence and nonexistence, nor that which is not at once existence and nonexistence."

Judaism also refused to name God, and simply referred to "Him" as YHWH, which means "I Am That I Am." God is Being itself, and the Kabalistic *Ain Soph*, in fact, means "nameless being."

Hindus have many names for the source of all Being, but each of them simply refers to different attributes of the Un-nameable One, or Brahman. Brahman, the Godhead, is composed of Brahma the Creator, Vishnu the Sustainer, and Shiva the Destroyer.

Manifest reality—the Universe—comes into being out of nothing, exists for a certain length of time (trillions of years) and is then destroyed—returning into a state of nothingness, or pure energy and potential—out of which another universe will eventually appear. According to Hinduism, this hide and seek game of God (lila) has been going on for eternity and will continue for eternity.

APPARENT DUALISM/
QUALIFIED NON-DUALISM

The relationship between the spiritual lover and Beloved is classical mystical language, but *our* reality *is* dualistic. I like to call this our "default reality." The way we normally perceive things is how the Universe reveals itself to us when we are in our "default" consciousness. From a practical point of view, we could not communicate, teach, learn, make love, write books, perform medical procedures, build houses, or even question our own existence if we did not live with the perception of separateness. Our perceived dualistic reality allows us to function as human beings.

Behind appearances, Buddhists and Hindus would argue, everything is ultimately empty of substance. Current quantum theory in physics seems to suggest the same thing. If we put aside for the moment the philosophical intricacies in Buddhist and Hindu thought on the subject, we see that both philosophies claim that while phenomena are real enough, ultimately phenomena are empty of substance. The phenomenal realm is essentially an illusion, or *maya*.

Ancient Gnostic-Christians came to this same realization. They, however, decided that the world of matter, including the human body, was not just apparent reality, but was essentially evil in nature. According

THE ESSENTIAL MYSTICS, POETS, SAINTS, AND SAGES

to them, matter was created by an evil demi-god. Gnostics considered the Creator God of the Bible to be evil because his motive for creating humanity was to trap divinity in flesh, and thereby rob us of our divine inheritance. Matter cloaks divinity, and as long as it exists we are led into believing that we are separate from the All.

Gnostics considered the "human condition" to be one of ignorance, not original sin. In Gnostic-Christianity, the Christ was sent forth from the Godhead to bring us *gnosis*, or knowledge, of our true nature and divine origin. Ignorance can be dispelled by knowledge. Once we learn that we are sparks of Eternal Light, our souls are freed to return home to the All.

The Gospel of Mary (Magdalene) describes the soul's final ascent:

> That which has bound me has been loosed. The walls that have surrounded me have been torn down. My desires (cravings) have ceased and my ignorance has ended. From this hour on, for the duration of this aeon, I will receive rest in silence.

Through the ages orthodox Christian scholars and theologians have referred to Gnostics as radical dualists. I believe this is a misperception. Gnostics, like Hindus and Buddhists, saw the material realm as essentially illusory. All things emanated from the All, and all things would eventually be resolved back into the All. In Reality, only the All exists. Again in *The Gospel of Mary*, Jesus almost echoes Buddha's teaching on dependent origination:

> Every nature, every modeled form, every creature, exists in and with each other. They will dissolve again into their proper root. For the nature of matter is dissolved into what belongs to its nature.

The Gnostic-Christian mystics understood the concept of *apparent* dualism as well, and called the pairs of opposites that make up the world of human

perception *syzgies*. Again and again in the Gnostic Gospels, Jesus sounds
almost like a Taoist, emphasizing the necessity of harmonizing "the two"
into the One. The concept of spiritual androgyny runs throughout Gnostic-Christian literature, and the message is that one must unify one's own
consciousness before it is possible to see that duality is ultimately illusory.
In *The Gospel of Thomas* Jesus states the doctrine plainly:

> When you make the two into one, and when you make that which
> is outside [you] like that which is inside [you] and when you make
> that which is above like that which is below (macrocosm and mi-
> crocosm) and when you make the male and the female into a single
> one [being] . . . then you will be able to enter the Kingdom.

The nature of things might be quite different in a parallel universe, but
in our universe virtually everything manifests itself in pairs of opposites:
night and day, good and evil, hate and love, wealth and poverty, darkness
and light, health and sickness, male and female. Even the human brain
is composed of two hemispheres—one analytical, the other intuitive:
masculine and feminine.

Pairs of opposites have male/female characteristics. *Yin* is feminine;
Yang is masculine. Tao is the intermixing of both, and the Tao would
not exist without both. Hindus use *Shiva* and *Shakti* to express the same
idea, yet understand that *Shiva* and *Shakti* are dualistic aspects of the one
monistic Brahman. Buddhists call this spiritual sexual pairing *Yab/Yum*.
In Hebrew, knowledge is masculine, while wisdom is feminine.

In orthodox Christianity—though few Christians realize it—the
Holy Spirit always appears in the original Greek of the *New Testament* as
feminine. The metaphorical goddess, Sofia, or wisdom, is also feminine.
In the Jewish *Kabbalah*, the female principle is known as the *Shekinah*.
The human need for the feminine principle is so strong that even in

patriarchal traditions like Roman Catholicism, the patriarchs were forced to re-invent Jesus' mother as an immaculate virgin (now the *Queen of Heaven*) in order to restore the lost feminine aspect to orthodoxy.

Gods and goddesses (consorts) are everywhere in religious mythology. Even though we live in the apparent world of duality, there is a strong human need to heal separateness. Contrary to what many women believe today, in ancient texts, the goddess almost never exists alone; she is nearly always the *consort* of the male principle—which is to say that neither the god nor the goddess can exist without the other.

Coupling metaphors run through all mystical traditions. The third century Gnostic *The Gospel of Philip* hints that the historical Mary Magdalene was considered a personification of *Sophia*, or *Wisdom* and was, therefore, a goddess and cosmic consort of the Christ. In Tibetan Buddhism, the historical Yeshe Tsogyel is considered to be the consort of Padmasambahva, the founder of Buddhism in Tibet.

At some deep primordial level we seem to understand this need for wholeness. We need the balance between the pairs of opposites. Non-dualism—androgyny—is the only thing that can overcome patriarchal bias and restore our gender balance that is so essential. In the material realm, however, the One always includes the Two.

Why is our universe manifested in this way? I think we can safely say that we'll never be able to answer the *why* question. But obviously we do not see ourselves as existing in the realm of pure Spirit. We *believe* that we do exist, however; and by all appearances, we do. And that is a paradox: in order to realize Ultimate Reality, we must (consciously) cease seeing ourselves as separate and apart—but without mystic insight, this is impossible.

Buddhists and Hindus believe that the phenomenal world is illusory, but many of them still live in houses, drive cars, go to work, and make love. The simple intellectual realization that only the One exists is obviously not sufficient for Enlightenment; nor is the mere belief that phenomenal reality is essentially an illusion.

The only way we can become whole and illumined is to altogether disengage the thinking mind and overcome the misapprehension that we are individual, separate beings—separate from each other and separate from the *One-Who-Is*.

Like Taoists, the ancient Buddhist philosopher Nagarjuna taught that "reality" exists in polarity. Everything exists in relationship to its opposite, and the opposites are continuously reversing poles. Modern science agrees: "Every action has an equal and opposite reaction."

Nagarjuna pointed out that shortness exists only in relation to the *idea* of length. "When bigness is present, smallness comes into being. When smallness is present, bigness comes to be. When evil arises, goodness comes to be; and when goodness arises, evil comes into being." This is a radical idea for most people, but it is the law of the universe: Goodness, in effect, *forces* evil into existence and vice versa. Every action has an equal, and opposite, reaction. Nagarjuna and Taoists both taught that these polarities are fixed and immutable.

According to the second law of thermodynamics, the universe—the cosmos as a whole—is a closed system, which means the laws within it never vary, and there is nothing outside a closed system that can affect those laws. In a closed system, disorder can never *decrease*, and order can never *increase*. According to quantum theory, the information that creates or maintains order must be constant. It can not increase or decrease, which means chaos cannot exist without an equal amount of order, and order cannot exist without an equal amount of chaos.

Thus, all polarities in relative understanding exist in perfect balance. The male cannot exist without the female and the "good" cannot exist without the "evil."

This concept is perfectly represented in the *Yin/Yang* symbol of the Tao: both polarities are constantly mutating into their opposites.

According to Hindus, a person's *karma* (action) is predetermined based upon his or her past karma. This is not fatalism or predestination; it is just the understanding that past karma influences who and what we are. If one becomes enlightened, then by definition one has already canceled one's past karma. Some Hindu philosophical systems argue that to act at all in the world once one is enlightened is counter-productive—it will only create new karma.

According to Taoism, Tao is simply what it is: a harmony of opposites which are always in a state of flux. Taoists have the philosophy of *wu wei*, which is best translated as "leaving things alone." To tamper with the *way-things-are* is to upset perfect balance; therefore Tao is disturbed. In an effort to change what is, say the Taoists, one can make things worse. To be in harmony with Tao is to make no effort, for effort upsets the perfect balance of Yin/Yang.

The rigid tree snaps in strong winds, while bamboo bends and thus survives. The continual resistance against negative things that come into our lives eventually becomes debilitating. Resistance is futile, and it can even drive us crazy. The ancient Taoist sages would tell us that we can only be happy in life if we accept, and not judge, that which changes—since change is inevitable.

Chuang Tzu, or Zhangzi, one of Taoism's greatest philosophers, was both a skeptic and a relativist, and the following short stories exemplify both:

Chuang Tzu and Huizi were walking by a dam when Chuang Tzu said, "See how the little fish are enjoying themselves, darting this way and that without a care."

Huizi replied, "How do you know the fish are enjoying themselves? You're not a fish."

Chuang Tzu countered with, "How do you know I don't know? You're not me!"

———∞∞∞———

Once Chuang Tzu dreamt that he was a butterfly flitting around, happy with himself, doing what he pleased. When Chuang Tzu suddenly woke up, he didn't know whether he was Chuang Tzu dreaming that he was a butterfly, or a butterfly dreaming that he was Chuang Tzu.

The philosophy of *Wu Wei* teaches that we should *act without acting*. When someone exerts his will against the world, he disrupts the primordial harmony. *Wu Wei* is not so much non-action as it is acting in harmony with the natural order of things.

Another related concept of Taoism is *P'u*, which encourages one to keep oneself in the primordial state of Tao. This is thought to be the true nature of the mind, unburdened by knowledge and experiences. In the state of *P'u*, there is no right or wrong, beautiful or ugly. There is only pure experience, or awareness, free from intellectual labels and definitions—pure potential, and perception without prejudice. In this state, everything can be seen as it truly is, without preconceptions or illusion. In this, Buddhists, Hindus, Sufi, and Christian mystics are all in agreement.

Ramana Maharshi once said, "There is nothing wrong with God's creation. Misery and suffering only exist in the mind." Uppaluri Gopala Krishnamurti expressed this same understanding less tactfully:

You want a different world so that you can be happy in it. . . Since you are determined to bring about change—a notion put into you by your culture—you remain discontent and want the world to be different. When your inner demand to be something different than what in fact you are comes to an end, the neurotic demand to change your society ceases. Then you cannot be in conflict with society; you are in perfect harmony with society, including its brutalities and miseries. All your attempts to change this brutal society only adds momentum to it.

(From: *Mind Is a Myth—Disquieting Conversations with a Man Called U.G.*).

PERCEPTION, COSMOLOGY, AND THE ONE

Buddhism and Advaita Vedanta are India's two great philosophical systems, and they have both similarities and differences. Shankara, the great Indian philosopher of Advaita Vedanta (un-qualified non-dualism), argued against the Buddha's idea of dependent origination and came up with a philosophy about existence that Vedantists believe supersedes the idea of dependent origination.

The Buddha proposed the concept of dependent origination to explain how things come into being, but Vedantist position is explained by Satischandra Chatterjee and Dhirendramohan Datta, in *An Introduction to Indian Philosophy:*

> Momentary things cannot possess any causality. Because to produce an effect, the cause must first arise and then act and, therefore, stay for more than one moment, which is against the doctrine of momentariness. Even if the separate momentary elements are somehow produced, no aggregate can be caused, for no substances are admitted by Buddhists which can bring together the elements and produce the desired objects. As consciousness itself is admitted to be the effect of the aggregation of different

elements, it cannot exist before aggregation, and the difficulty of unconscious cause arises.

Both Hindus and Buddhists believe in maya, or illusion, but in slightly different ways. Chatterjee and Datta state that Vedanta has a different perspective from the Buddhist idea of subjective idealism.

> They err when they declare that the world, like a dream, is only an illusory product of one's imagination. And yet, the existence of external objects cannot be denied since they are perceived to exist by all persons. If what we experience before us is disbelieved, then even the reality of mental states cannot be believed in.
>
> To say that ideas of the mind are illusory and only appear real is meaningless unless at least something external is admitted to be real. There are, of course, substantial differences between dream-objects and perceived objects. The first are contradicted by waking experience, while the latter are not.

External objects perceived during waking experience cannot be said to be unreal since we act as if they are. So subjective idealism, and along with it, nihilism (*sunyavada*) fail to explain the world in a satisfactory manner. Even the insights of current physics seem paradoxical. Ervin Laszlo in his book, *Science and the Akashic Field: An Integral Theory of Everything*, states:

> The view that space is empty and passive, and not even real to boot, is diametrically opposed to the view we get at the leading edge of science. What the new physics describes as the unified vacuum—the seat of all fields and forces of the physical world— is in fact the most fundamentally real element of the universe. Out of it have sprung the particles that make up our universe, and when black holes "evaporate," it is into it that the particles

fall back again. What we think of as matter is but the quantized, semi-stable bundling of energies that spring from the vacuum. In the last count, matter is but a waveform disturbance in the quasi-infinite energy-and in-formation-sea that is the connecting field, and the enduring memory, of the universe.

Where does all this leave us? We're stuck with paradox: the phenomenal realm is both real and unreal simultaneously.

But physics agrees to a certain point that behind the world of appearances, there is only emptiness. All things are ultimately devoid of substance. All substance is empty of form. The mystic who "wakes up" recognizes that dualism is the result of his or her own dualistic mind. Heal the split in our own consciousness, and the world is seen anew.

Catherine of Siena said, "The soul dwells like a fish in the sea, and the sea in the fish."

Nothingness is held within the paradox of everythingness. Nagarjuna argued that the concept that everything exists is one extreme, while the concept of nothingness is the other. Therefore it is necessary to take the middle way between the two extremes. His ultimate answer: abandon all views.

When my mind becomes Your mind, what is left to remember? Once my life is Your gesture, how can I pray? When all my awareness is Yours, what is there to know? I became You, Lord, and forgot You.

—MAHADEVIYAKKA

The female Catholic mystic Hadewijch of Antwerp put it this way:

God makes known to you, dear child, who He is and how He treats his servants . . . how he consumes them within Himself.

From the depths of this wisdom He shall teach you what He is and with what wonderful sweetness the One Lover comes to live in the other and so permeates the other that they do not know themselves from each other. But they possess themselves from each other, in mutual delight. Mouth to mouth, heart in heart, body in body, soul in soul, while a single divine nature flows within them both.

The author of *The Gospel of Philip* put these words into the mouth of the Christ, the Savior:

I came to make the things below like the things above. And those things without, like those within. I came to make them One.

Sacred language is often difficult to understand, since scripture often makes no distinction between history and mythology. The "consort," for example, is more than an individual goddess—she is the embodiment of the *feminine principle* itself.

John of the Cross said, "For, in order to conquer all the desires and to deny itself the pleasures which it has in everything, and for which its love and affection are wont to enkindle the will that it may enjoy them, it would need to experience another and a greater enkindling by another and a better love, which is that of its Spouse."

In the world of religious mythology, coupling is a metaphor for union with the Absolute. The yab/yum (father/mother) in Tantric Buddhism represents the union of wisdom and compassion. The practice of sexual Tantra is meant to produce a mystical experience of union and dissolve the false duality of subject/object.

For the Greek philosopher Plotinus, the One was beyond all attributes including being and non-being. Although the One is the source of the world, it did not willfully create the world. Apparent reality simply emanated from the One, since the One Itself is unchangeable.

Does our mind produce the phenomena with which we interact? In his book, *The Private Sea, LSD and the Search for God*, William Braden experienced (on LSD) the loss of self-identity and union with the One. For him the experience was entirely negative. His mind was not prepared for what it encountered.

As his mystical consciousness began to dawn, Braden felt like he was awakening from an episode of amnesia. What he had forgotten, he suddenly remembered—and wished he had not. Gradually he began to remember who he really was: Life, Being itself.

> Having been reunited with the Ground of my Being, I wanted urgently to be estranged from it again as quickly as possible. . .
>
> I had lost God but had gained the whole universe. . . and that was more than I could cope with. . . I could sense there was that which resisted both its Being and Becoming. And this something was nothing more than Nothingness itself, against which the Self had exerted its will to Become. . . .
>
> Now I thought that I knew the truth: the deadly and unbearable truth that nobody created us . . . we created ourselves.

For Braden, the response to the experience of union was one of existential terror:

> For along with [the loss of] my own self I had lost all the other selves as well. I had lost other people. And I missed them very much. I wanted there to be someone else. Anyone else. And if there had been just two of us—really two of us—and we two were All That There Was—that would not have been so hard. But there was no one else; there was only the One.

Braden had walked through the looking glass and plunged down the rabbit hole without any preparation, and the experience terrified him. He was unable to face the discovery of *Ultimate Being* calmly because he lacked the requisite years of spiritual discipline that are necessary to prepare the individual for an otherwise shocking revelation.

An Eastern spiritual master might have told him that LSD forced all his chakras to open at once, which allowed the serpent force of *Kundalini* to shoot up through him in an instant and literally blow his mind.

There are other perils on the path of the mystic. There are stops along the way to Enlightenment, and mystics may find themselves in states of consciousness so blissful that going any further seems pointless. Teresa of Avila disagreed:

> When they [mystics] experience any spiritual consolation, therefore, their physical nature is too much for them; and as soon as they feel any interior joy there comes over them a physical weakness and languor, and they fall in a sleep, which they call "spiritual," and which is a little more marked than the condition that has been described. Thinking the one state to be the same as the other, they abandon themselves to this absorption, and the more they relax, the more complete becomes this absorption, because their physical nature continues to grow weaker. So they get it into their heads that it is *arrobamiento*, or rapture. But I call it *abobamiento*, foolishness; for they are doing nothing but wasting their time at it and ruining their health.

THE NARROW GATE

Enter by the narrow gate; for the gate is wide and the way is easy, that leads to destruction, and those who enter by it are many. For the gate is narrow and the way is hard, that leads to life, and those who find it are few.

—MATTHEW 7:13-14

These words of Jesus describe the choice we all have to make in life. The mass of humanity always chooses the wide gate because it leads to an enormous playground of sensual fun and enjoyable opportunities—until it becomes clear that there is nothing in the world of matter that provides permanent happiness—since everything is, by nature, impermanent. In the end, craving leads to suffering.

Those throughout history who have found and chosen to open the narrow gate, and take the road less traveled are very rare beings. They are the bravest men and women who have ever walked the planet because instead of setting out to conquer the world—which would be far easier in comparison—they seek to conquer themselves instead.

The two gates, the two paths, are always open to all of us, yet the narrow gate is quite unattractive to most. It lacks glitter, bling, shiny bright new things. Choosing it is counter-intuitive. The narrow gate opens onto a path of rigorous discipline, material deprivation, and constant inner struggle. No wonder so few choose the hero's journey when just living a normal life is hard enough.

Even so, the great mystics of all ages wanted more than a mere pot of gold at the end of a rainbow; more than riches, power, a yacht, and a private jet. They wanted more than fame and recognition, a place in history. They even wanted more than family, friends, and great sex. They wanted, instead, the pearl of great price, the jewel within the lotus. They wanted true peace of mind, true freedom, bliss consciousness, and the perpetual ecstasy that comes with the realization of one's essential union with the All. They wanted the greatest treasure in life: to become enlightened; to become liberated from human suffering; to become one with the All. They wanted a heart so open with love and compassion that it included every living thing.

The mere fact that you are reading these words, and I am writing them, means that you and I want what the great mystics of the past wanted. If there was a pill that we could take that would cleanse the lenses of our perception and allow us to instantly *wake up*, no doubt many of us would not hesitate to swallow it.

Unfortunately, there is no such pill. There is only that narrow gate which opens to a path that is unimaginably difficult to walk. So we hesitate at the gate's latch, play with it, lubricate it, swing the gate back and forth, and then paint it so that it will look nice. We may even stick our toes under the gate just to see what the path feels like. Even for those of us who are not yet ready to take the final journey, the path beckons nonetheless.

In our own defense, we argue that we have already come a great distance, survived uncountable struggles, and endured much suffering through many incarnations just to *find* the narrow gate—just to realize

that there is another way to lead one's life. You and I have already realized truths about life and the nature of reality that most of humanity isn't even aware of, or couldn't care less about.

The day is coming, and we know it, when we *will* have the courage to open the gate and take our first step on the narrow path. In the meantime, we are preparing for this final journey in life by putting more useful things into our backpack and getting rid of more and more things we don't need.

I think it is significant that in the case of both Siddhartha Gautama (the historical Buddha) and Jesus of Nazareth, the mythology of temptation by Mara the evil one, and Satan, respectively, is so similar. Both myths make it clear that each man had to pass a final test—the last temptations. *The-one-who-is-not-God*—that which is in our own minds—offered them the world and all of its power and glitter if they would just renounce their silly quest for ultimate truth. But Siddhartha vanquished Mara, and Jesus vanquished Satan; and in doing so they became brothers: Siddhartha became the Buddha (awakened one) and Jesus became the Christ.

These two spiritual heroes, like many others whose words are recorded in this book—both men and women—wanted something far more precious than could be found on the road that is accessed through the wide gate. They wanted freedom from this veil of tears we call life.

And yet we today face even greater challenges than they did. Humanity has invented things that we no longer know how to live without: electricity, telephones, computers, automobiles. We could run away and join a monastic community, but nowadays a monastery may have the Internet, electricity, indoor plumbing, and automobiles.

These are times in which we must somehow transcend all of this, and yet we don't know how. Only the Perennial Philosophy offers a way out, and that way begins nowhere else but inside of us. In the *Theologia Germanica* we read:

> The two eyes of the soul of man cannot both perform their work at once: but if the soul shall see with the right eye into eternity, then the left eye must close itself and refrain from working, and be as though it were dead. For if the left eye be fulfilling its office toward outward things, that is holding converse with time and the creatures; then must the right eye be hindered in its work; that is, in its contemplation. Therefore, whoever will have the one must let the other go; for no man can serve two masters.

THE NATURE OF MYSTICAL EXPERIENCE

Ineffability

A most significant effect of the mystical experience is the inability to put the mystical experience into words. Direct awareness is needed to understand the mystic insight.

States of mind are not easily transferable from one level of perception to another. Many years ago, when I first tried marijuana, I thought I had some very brilliant insights about life. The insights came faster than I could write them down. What a shock it was the next morning when I read what I had written the night before; it was all gibberish. I couldn't make heads or tails of anything I wrote. I knew that my insights of the previous night were absolutely valid, but I was unable to communicate them—even to myself.

Noetic Quality

Successful mystics claim to have attained gnosis, pure knowledge of the Absolute—a Reality that cannot be accessed by the discursive mind. Such illuminations themselves may fade in normal states of consciousness, but their profound effect does not. Once a view of the Absolute is achieved, it is not soon forgotten. While true knowledge cannot be articulated to anyone else, one's new understanding carries the weight of authority from then on.

Transiency

Usually, the mystical state of awakened awareness cannot be maintained. Almost certainly that would be true for those who achieve "mini" enlightenments. But Hindus and Buddhists both maintain that true Enlightenment is a state of consciousness that is permanent. This seems to mean that an illuminated being like the Buddha would have the ability to function simultaneously in more than one reality.

Passivity

Although entering a mystical state is usually voluntary and intentional, once the state is achieved, the one experiencing it has the sense that his or her own will is in abeyance—that one's whole being is sublimated to a higher power. "Not my will, but Thine be done," or as the Apostle, Paul, put it: "No longer I, but Christ in me." Such a state of mind always produces a memory of that state of mind, even when one returns to *default* reality.

THE HUMAN CONDITION

Ignorance and Craving

Eastern philosophers have a great deal to say about ignorance; not intellectual ignorance, but spiritual ignorance. Most people believe that the way they perceive the world is the only way it can be perceived; that belief is due to ignorance.

But now, even physics suggests that nothing is really solid. Behind the appearance of solidity are masses of swirling atoms—with a lot of space between them. Solidity is only the appearance, not the nature, of a thing. If we believe that the appearance of something is the only reality, we are trapped in ignorance.

Hinduism and Buddhism tell us that this sort of ignorance is precisely what keeps us tied to *samsara*, the wheel of birth, death, and rebirth. To escape that wheel we must come to understand the true nature of things. On this subject Krishna in The Bhagavad Gita states:

Men of understanding think of Me, the Unmanifest as having Manifestation, not knowing My higher nature, changeless and Supreme.

Veiled by my creative power, I am not revealed to all. This bewildered world knows Me not, the unborn, the unchanging. I

THE ESSENTIAL MYSTICS, POETS, SAINTS, AND SAGES

know the beings that are past, that are present . . . and that are to come, but Me no one knows.

All beings are born deluded . . . overcome by the dualities which arise from desire and hate . . . But those men of virtuous deeds in whom sin has come to an end, freed from the delusion of dualities, worship Me steadfast in their vows. Those who take refuge in Me, and strive for deliverance from old age and death—they know the Brahman [the Absolute] entire; they know Atman [the Self] . . .

Those who know Me as the One that governs the material and divine aspects . . . with their minds harmonized, have knowledge of Me even at the time of their departure from here.

In ancient Gnosticism, all Gnostic sects were intent on dispelling ignorance and replacing it with "gnosis," or "knowledge." They were not seeking intellectual knowledge; they were trying to dispel spiritual ignorance. In the Gnostic-Christian text *Thomas the Contender*, Jesus states:

How sad it is for you who hope in the flesh, and are attached to the prison (the physical body) that will perish. How long will you remain in ignorance? Your hope is in this world. Your god is this life. You are corrupting your souls.

Ignorance leads to our grasping for what the flesh desires: good food, sex, wealth, power, family, fun, beauty, and on and on. As long as craving has its fangs sunk into us we cannot see what lies beyond materialism. Overwhelmed by our lust for things and feelings, we do not even realize that it is the craving itself that causes our suffering. Ignorance is the nonrecognition of what the problem really is, and that there is a solution to the problem.

The Buddha pointed out that even happiness itself will lead to suffering because we will eventually lose what makes us happy—the house, the car, the kids, the spouse, our own life. All things that give us pleasure now will eventually cause us pain. Unless one gives up attachment to all things, and ends craving for things of this world, suffering will always continue. The Buddha prescribed the Four Noble Truths and the Noble Eight-fold Path as a cure, while Jesus stated, "Seek first the kingdom of God and all things will be added unto you." Different words, same teaching.

Often people don't see craving for what it is. Craving a drug or a candy bar are obvious examples. But there are subtle cravings as well: the mother who is not happy if she does not have her daughter's love; the father who is disappointed unless his sons are good at sports; the grandmother who is dissatisfied unless her grandchildren succeed in life. We crave good health, world peace, and even Enlightenment itself. But the mystics of all ages tell us that *all* cravings, all desires—including the desire to "wake up"—must be eliminated if we are to attain true freedom in this life. As the Buddha said, "Want nothing until you need nothing."

THE WAY OF THE MYSTIC

Desire, Attachment, and Renunciation

The first step through the narrow gate requires that the mystic renounce the world. I know of no enlightened being who has not done so. It was the first step for the Buddha, the first step for Jesus, the first step for St. Francis, the first step for Gandhi.

These individuals did not renounce the world because they considered it evil like the Gnostics did. They became renunciates because they wanted their attachment to things to cease. They saw through the curtain of illusion which is the material world. Liberation from craving and attachment ends the game. When the game is finished for good, all that remains is the One; and the One is in need of nothing.

Concentrating and Controlling the Mind: Introspection and Quietude

Whether in the form of meditation or prayer, silence is a great teacher. Without retreat from the world, whether full time or part time, one cannot work on quieting and focusing the mind, and emptying it of thoughts. The essential work of every mystic in this regard is identical. Anyone who has ever tried to meditate knows how difficult it is to empty oneself of thoughts. I like the term "monkey mind" to describe the

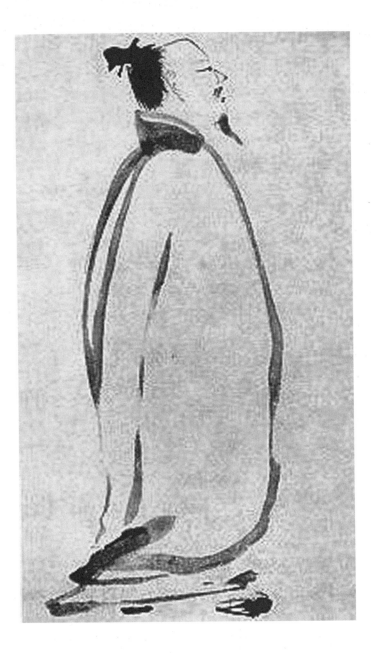

mind's incessant insistence on being heard. Controlling this chatter is very hard work, and eliminating it entirely takes many years of practice. It really doesn't matter why the mind does what it does; beginning the practice of quieting it is all anyone needs to know. But perhaps knowing the cause would help us to recognize what's going on. Sit in meditation and wait for monkey mind to begin its distractive and disruptive chatter. When thoughts interfere with your empty mind, what form do they take? Are they visual, or are they linguistic?

Monkey mind loves words and cannot exist without words—language. Your silent mind is constantly being interrupted with ideas constructed with words. Words that rattle around in our heads keep us from seeing what is—now. What was human consciousness before Homo sapiens invented language? Did we perceive reality directly, without judgment, like a baby does? It seems that as soon as we learn to speak and write, our minds turn away from direct awareness and focus more on mere symbols of awareness: words.

Metaphorically, I think Homo sapiens' "fall from grace," our break with the natural world [the "Garden of Eden"] began at the moment we developed language. Once we began communicating with each other with abstract symbols, the thinking mind came into being. Once we started thinking in words we started philosophizing, debating, and annoying one another.

Our disagreements then led us to judgments about reality, no longer experiencing it directly. If we are to reverse the process, then shutting down the analytical mind is necessary. This is what Jesus meant when he said, "You must be born again. You must become like a little child."

To train the mind to cease its constant harassment of thoughts, we need a means—a technique—to overcome it. That's where meditation comes in. Virtually all mystics would agree that quieting the mind, and emptying it of thoughts, is absolutely essential for spiritual progress. It is the first step and every step thereafter—until there is a breakthrough.

Unfortunately, meditation is not a fast track to Enlightenment. One may practice for many years before discovering the full value of meditation. Until we do, meditation is an act of faith. But the mystics tell us that eventually meditation will lead to direct awareness.

Another method of quieting the mind is through the use of "mantra." This is a way of using words against themselves to block out the flow of linguistic thought. Since mantra is the constant repetition of a word or phrase, it blocks out abstract thinking. The more adept you get in practicing mantra, the quieter your mind will become.

A small book I read many years ago, *The Way of the Pilgrim*, was written by an anonymous Russian monk. The text somehow found its way to a monastery in Greece during the nineteenth century, and the monks subsequently published it. The main character in the story is "the pilgrim." Everywhere this wanderer went he repeated what some call the *Jesus Prayer:* "Jesus have mercy, Christ have mercy."

After years of repeating this mantra, the pilgrim was rewarded not only with serenity and peace of mind, but also with a grateful heart filled with love for all those he encountered—not a bad recommendation for the use of a mantra.

There are two thoughts on the practice of mantra. One is that it doesn't matter what word or phrase one uses. No matter what it is, it will still work to quiet the mind. But others say that the words you repeat send out subtle vibrations that affect both our minds and the world around us, so the proper words are important. Ancient tradition holds that a mantra should be given to you by your teacher. But if you don't have a formal teacher, listen to the infallible teacher that resides in your own heart. If you pick a popular Hindu/Buddhist mantra like "Om mani padme hum," (Om, the jewel is in the lotus, Om) you can't go wrong.

Mantra is often used in conjunction with prayer beads or "malas." It is interesting that most all religious traditions independently developed the use of these beads in order to keep count of their repetitions. Even though the count itself is unimportant, it helps one to discipline oneself by setting goals to repeat the mantra x number of times a day. Plus, the mala's presence is a reminder, like a string tied round a finger, to keep practicing. Hindus, Buddhists, Sufis, and Roman Catholics all use a form of prayer beads. While Judaism generally considers these to be pagan, the Hebrew prayer shawl, the *tallit*, is knotted with a specific number of knots as a remembrance of the commandments of the Lord and may be used in the same way as a mala is used.

Eliminating Attraction and Aversion

Things and people either attract or repel us, and as long as that is the case—as long as our minds distinguish between this and that—we make judgments: This is good, that is bad. We create our own duality, and as long as the mind is split this way, we cannot achieve peace of mind. How do we disentangle ourselves from seeing some people and some things as beautiful, and other people and other things as ugly or repugnant?

St. Francis' ministry to lepers provides a useful example. Overcome aversion by embracing what is repugnant to you. Overcome attraction by denying yourself gratification.

Jesus counseled against making distinctions between people—even "good" and "evil" people: "The Father allows the rain to fall on the just and unjust alike." In the words of the Third Chinese Patriarch of Zen:

The Way is perfect, like vast space where nothing is lacking. Nothing is in excess. Indeed, it is due to our choosing to accept or reject that we do not see the true nature of things. Live neither in the entanglements of outer things, nor in inner feelings of emptiness. Be serene in the oneness of things, and such erroneous views will disappear by themselves.

Mindfulness: Living in the Present Moment

Mindfulness—living fully in the present moment, and living the moment fully—is not just Buddhist philosophy, but is taught in all mystical philosophies. For Taoism, in particular, living this life, this moment *now* is the most beneficial response to life.

"Be here now" was a phrase first made popular by Ram Dass back in the 1960s. But what does it mean to be here now? It means living in the moment, focusing only on what is in front of us, and giving up thoughts about past and future.

When our mind is engaged in thinking about past events and events anticipated in the future, we are not fully present in the moment. We cannot perceive what is right in front of us because we are distracted with what is un-real: the past, which no longer exists, and the future that doesn't exist at all.

If we *think*, we are not here now, not fully present, because our mind is split—part of it is here, part of it is somewhere else. With half of our mind engaged elsewhere, we miss what is real in the now. This *now*, this present moment, will never come again, so why not give it our full attention?

According to theoretical physicist and astronomer Julian Barbour, time really doesn't exist. In his book *The End of Time*, he argues that the recognition that time does not exist will be the next revolution in physics. It will shock us. It will even cast doubt on Einstein's greatest contribution, the idea of a space-time continuum. In Barbour's opinion, the coming revolution in physics is going to turn our understanding about reality inside-out.

The Loss of the Affective Ego

Renouncing the world seems like it would be incredibly hard, and renouncing the ego seems entirely impossible. Modern society is especially challenged: we have iPhones and iPods, Facebook, YouTube, Twitter, and *American Idol*. We all deserve our fifteen minutes of fame. It is especially difficult to become nobody in a world that only respects those with strong egos.

The mystics tell us, however, that we can never realize we are one with the All until we have eradicated our personal sense of "I." God can't come to visit unless we're *not* home. As Ram Dass put it, "The [mystical] game is not about becoming *somebody*, it's about becoming *nobody*." In the mystic vision the sense of "I" dissolves and then there is only the One. How many of us are ready for *that*?

What would it mean to lose the affective ego and the energy that animates it? What would it be like to lose that which sets into motion the search for gratification? In losing the affective ego, it will seem that all of the energy we're used to has disappeared. It has just drained out and gone elsewhere.

Imagine the ego as a room with four doors. Each door represents a particular way our ego functions. If we were to use Jungian terminology, we might call these doors "sensation," "intuition," "thinking," and "feeling."

On any given day, the room of ego is full of all kinds of activity. People are coming in and out of the doors. We watch them do what they do. There is always something going on—and we not only experience it, but relate to it. That which animates this activity is the ego, as it is alive and always seeking out things that are pleasurable and avoiding things that are painful. All of this takes place automatically.

One day, however, we might suddenly find that the room is empty. The ego energy that set everything in motion has suddenly disappeared. We will be disoriented and wonder what's happened. Everything we knew about life has disappeared along with the ego.

Even what we believed life itself to be has disappeared. What happened? Did someone lock all the doors? No. The doors still open and close, but nobody is coming in and out, and we even have to open the doors ourselves—which takes will power just to carry on our daily affairs.

Ego is still there. It is not cognitively impaired. All the abilities and skills we have learned in life are still with us, but the ego has gone off to some place of silence where it no longer pays attention to the usual noise of its activity. Now there seems to be no need to seek out things and people.

The loss of ego can happen rather suddenly, so it is quite noticeable. Normal life has disappeared and cannot be regained. Thus when the ego disappears, it is a kind of death, and the ego might mourn its death and the life it no longer has.

In this new state of being, the ego is no longer affected by desires. Just to function takes an act of will. That which formerly attracted us ceases to exist. One may also feel a sense of worthlessness, that there is nothing worth doing. There is an emptiness inside.

The Dark Night of the Soul

Such is the nature of the soul before Enlightenment that it undergoes a dark night. Not only has the ego-self disappeared, but in the emptiness, the mystic doubts everything. Worse, the

presence of the divine ceases to exist, and that is the hardest thing of all.

You are ravished, as if in darkness, and know not what you do or don't do. You do not even know if you exist or not. And you wonder if you will perish.

—JUAN FALCONI

The Dark Night of the Soul was written by John of the Cross, and describes his own dark night—the darkest hour, right before dawn. It is the period of emptiness and doubt that proceeds illumination, though the mystic cannot yet see it. Discouragement is common. The questions are likely to be: Have I wasted my life for nothing? Has everything I've done been pointless?

The mystic comes to the end of his or her journey, and just before the breakthrough, doubt and despair set in. Then on the distant horizon, dawn breaks and Light begins to illuminate everything.

You cannot see the light unless you stand in the darkness!

—JESUS, *DIALOGUE OF THE SAVIOR*

Considering all the perils and pitfalls, difficult work, and tremendous faith needed, it is not hard to understand why so few people take the mystic's journey. Even so, we have a yearning for what these brave men and women found on their path because we intuit that life has to be more meaningful than it seems to be for most of us, most of the time. We think, *Is this all there is? Is this as good as it gets? Life is hard, then you die?*

All too many people answer "yes" to these questions and would call themselves realists. When you're dead you're dead, and there is no real point to life. So, eat, drink, and be merry.

This is not the truth that I hold in my own heart, and since you are reading this book it is likely that this is not your truth either. One day, perhaps not in this incarnation, I will finally open the narrow gate myself. I will offer up my fear to *That-Which-Is* and take the first bold step on the road less traveled. Should I meet you on the way, I might not recognize you as you, or me as me. It is possible that all I will see is . . . the One.

There is nothing to do
But sit, looking for your own
Hand in front of your face.
Through the thick black dark
In the cave of the heart where the
Self sleeps, dreamless and still.

—TERE OUWEHAND

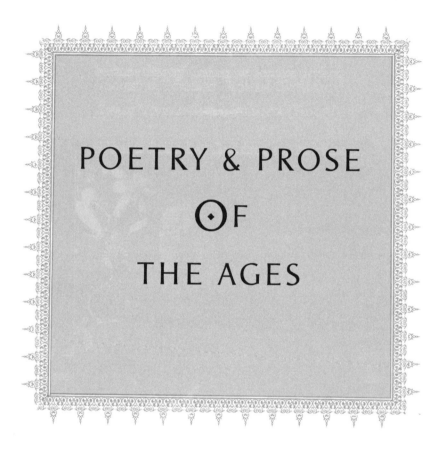

POETRY & PROSE

OF

THE AGES

THE BELOVED

In the beginning, before spirit and matter were separated,
"here" and "there" had no meaning in existence.
There was no separation between the lover and the Beloved.
Only love existed.

TAKHRUDDIN IRAQI, SUFI

The moon was a mirror for me
to see myself and You, Blessed One.
I now realize that I am one and the same as you.
You are my first love.

THICH NHAT HANH, ZEN BUDDHIST

If only I could celebrate You
as a holiday that lasts a lifetime.
All my offerings to you are insignificant.
So is my adoration. What can I do, then?
I can go to and fro being a living witness—
to show You that I care.

RABBI ABRAHAM JOSHUA HESCHEL, JEWISH

The Beloved gives us the water of life,
which cures every illness.
In the Beloved's rose garden of Oneness,
no thorns survive.
I have heard it said that there is a window
between one heart to another.
But what supports the window
if walls have ceased to exist?

JELALUDDIN RUMI, SUFI

The bride comes to the garden of her desires,
and there she rests in joy,
embraced in the arms of her Beloved.

THOMAS A' KEMPIS, ROMAN CATHOLIC

One cannot break the love that
connects You with me, Beloved.
Just as a diamond which
cannot be broken with a hammer,
my love for You is unbreakable.
My heart enters you as shine enters gold,
My heart resides in You as a lotus resides in water.
I get lost in You like a bird gets lost in the night sky.
Come again to me, Beloved.

MIRABAI, VEDANTA (HINDU)

How do I see the Beloved?
Not with my eyes, but with His.
For He can only see Himself.

MUHYADDIN IBN' ARIBI, SUFI

Drunk on love for the Beloved,

I wandered in the wilderness,

though I have no memory of anything.

There I learned the living knowledge of oneness.

When I forgot and forgot everything else,

I lost everything else.

Then the Beloved came to me

as the bridegroom to the bride.

THOMAS A' KEMPIS, ROMAN CATHOLIC

I have no use of this heart, Beloved,

unless it is for You.

Either give back my heart, or return to me.

ABU-SAID ABIL-KHEIR, SUFI

I dreamed that I came to your Temple, Lord.
There I praised those who sacrificed
their hearts to you.
You became manifest to me.
No longer did you appear as a mystery.
Then I awoke and found
that I was still with You,
and delighted in Your presence.

JUDAH HALEVI, JEWISH

Though it is difficult, I try to find
the One in the many—
the essence of unity
between the separateness of phenomena,
and the One who exists in all things—
the Beloved who dwells in everyone.

Often I fail in my efforts
when I cannot find the balance
between the seeming separateness
of things and their essential unity.
During those times, I feel afraid.
But make the effort anyway.

RAM DASS, VEDANTA (HINDU)

As one who loved the Beloved,
the Beloved took care of me.
He quenched my thirst, filled my stomach
and gave me love and patience.
He clothed me with humility
and cured me with truth.

RAMON LLULL, ROMAN CATHOLIC

I found God when I found love,
and it is this love that gives me strength
from one day to the next.
Love shows me the path I must take.

I am on fire
and I am the fuel that feeds the fire.
I am the smoke that proceeds from the fire.
Love made me aware of the Beloved.

SULTAN BAHU, SUFI

There is nothing this body and soul wants
but the Beloved. What else is left?
The Beloved is everything to me—
my successes, my failures, my life itself.
Without You, nothing has meaning.
When you laid claim to me, I gave myself to You.

So do with me what you will, Beloved.
I am yours.
I found you hiding within my own mind,
and the grace of that discovery saved me
from sinking into the sea of illusion.

RAMANA MAHARSHI, VEDANTA (HINDU)

I have found that which is priceless,
and accepted it as grace.
I have found the beginning of my rebirths,
while I have lost the rest of the world.
Thou art the Ocean of Love,
but the fetters of this life had separated
my love from You.
I lost myself and found the Beloved.

ABU-SAID ABIL-KHEIR, SUFI

Come to me at dawn, Beloved, and walk with me.

My soul is thirsty to see the children of my people.

Here in my inner room you have placed a seat of gold,

and a table set for You.

I am your bread.

I am the wine from my own vineyard.

Delight in drinking of me,

and may my taste be pleasing to you.

SOLOMON 'IBN GABIROL, JEWISH

The light of my Beloved cannot be seen

with these physical eyes.

I have taken upon myself all the sorrows of humanity.

I have loved this world,

but my love has been in the service of the Friend.

He barely touched me,

yet he kindled the fire in my heart.

Men want to confine the Beloved in their holy places,

but they cannot keep Him there.

Those who have eyes to see, see the Beloved everywhere.

DARSHAN SINGH, VEDANTA (HINDU)

Remove me from myself,
so that all that remains is you, Beloved.
Take my life so that I can stand in your Presence.
Let all that remains be You.

HALLAJ, SUFI

Everything that gives me life—
my heart, my mind, my feelings—
those things that I thought were mine, are Yours.
For I have given them to you completely.

LADIMIR SOLOVYOV, RUSSIAN ORTHODOX

Nothing exists but You, Beloved.
You are my speech. You are the silence of my mind.
You sleep with me. You walk the path with me.
There is nowhere I can go where You are not.
I have disappeared. Only You remain.

BULLEH SHAH, SUFI

We are mere drops in the ocean of truth,
floating atop the waves are bubbles that attract us
and want to seize us and keep us captive
in the sea of illusion.
If only a mere drop,
I ask to be brought to the shore of the Beloved.
I ask that the waves that keep us apart be banished.
May I see nothing else but the Beloved.

FRANCIS BRABAZON, SUFI

I would like an entire lifetime to praise You—
not just a holiday now and then.
My offerings to You and my adoration are small gifts,
hardly noticeable.
Would that I could wander here and there
and do nothing else but be a witness to You.
Still, that would be nothing more than a witness to my devotion.

RABBI ABRAHAM JOSHUA HESCHEL, JEWISH

This fortune, the Beloved,
cannot be spent and no one can steal it.
Each day it increases in value.
As I came across the ocean of existence,
the boatman was my true teacher.

MIRABAI, VEDANTA (HINDU)

I have forgotten all of Creation.
Only the Creator remains.
I have turned my attention
to that which is within me.
It is there where I am in love
with the Beloved.

JOHN OF THE CROSS, ROMAN CATHOLIC

The lover of the Beloved
is the bride who rests in the garden
of her yearning.
There she is joyous, for she is embraced
by the arms of the Beloved.

THOMAS A' KEMPIS, ROMAN CATHOLIC

They ask me,
"Who do you serve
and whose message do you deliver?"
And I tell them that I am a servant of the Beloved.

MANDAEN PRAYER, GNOSTIC

Everywhere I go,
from one end of the earth to another,
I find Him.
I see Him everywhere in the heavens.
I am the seeker, but when I see the Beloved,
the seeker disappears—
for I see Him with the eyes of my heart.
For those with eyes to see, the Beloved is everywhere.
He escapes those temples, mosques and churches
where they try to imprison Him.

DARSHAN SINGH, VEDANTA (HINDU)

My lover has a gentle nature.
He is immeasurable,
and alone is worthy of praise.
I cannot help but speak of His beauty,
for He has not hidden Himself from me.
But who can I tell? The angels, perhaps?
Certainly they are the only ones
who can speak such things.

You have taken me in Your arms, Beloved.
You have given me the greatest treasure of all:
the gift of Yourself.

MARGUERITE PORETE, ROMAN CATHOLIC

Call me to me, and I will run to you, never tiring.
You are my heavenly Spouse, and I will not rest
until You embrace me and support me,
and kiss me with the happiness of Your mouth.

CLARE OF ASSISI, ROMAN CATHOLIC

Throughout all of my travels, Friend,
you feed me until my journey ends.
You are my companion on the path,
my breath, my hope.
And it is You who gives me joy.
It is You who feeds my hunger,
and You who walks with me to my journey's end.
You alone do I long for.
You alone are my treasure.
You alone are my life and my love,
for without You I could not have wandered the world.
You have done so much for me through your grace—
so many favors, so many gifts.
I seek your love everywhere, and suddenly,
I am filled with it.
You dwell in my heart.
You are the glow in my eyes.
And my soul has but one desire:
to be one with You.

NACHMANIDES (RABBI MOSHE BEN NACHMAN), JEWISH

When he stripped me of my new clothes,
I lost all inhibitions.
He was all around me at night like an insect
circling a lotus.
Like a bird that flies up to the clouds,
in his freedom,
this God of love does not delay.

I remember some of the absurd tricks He played on me, as desire made
my heart burn with restlessness. Still, I was filled with fear.

VIDYAPATI, VEDANTA (HINDU)

In the light the lovers learn from the Beloved
how to catch on fire.
It is the fire that allows the moth to enter.
The gift of love is a gift that comes from the Beloved.

ABU-SAID ABIL-KHEIR, SUFI

I sing with a voice

that is as vast as the ocean itself.

The song produces all sounds and countless words,

and I will sing it through all cycles of time to come.

It is a song of praise to the ocean of love

that exists in the depths of the Buddha's heart.

GREAT KAMO PRIESTESS SENSHI, ZEN BUDDHIST

I want to be one with Him, but He insists

on being separate from Me.

Thus, I will abandon my desire to His will.

Everything the Beloved does comes from love,

so what is a poor lover to do?

I have no words, so I must give up both

my feeling of separation and my desire for union.

I become free of both, simply accepting

the Beloved's love.

TAKHRUDDIN IRAQI, SUFI

Those who burn themselves up in the
fire of the Beloved, no longer need
knowledge, intellect and religion.
They have left everything behind,
including themselves.
This is the meaning of the words,
"Blessed are the poor," for the poor
have nothing but the Beloved.

ABU-SAID ABIL-KHEIR, SUFI

"They reproach me about my relationship with the Beloved.
"How are the two of you getting along?" they ask sarcastically.
"The Beloved is mine," I say, "and the rest is none of your business."

NESIMI, SUFI

Love rushes through me
as if it were blood coursing in my veins.
It destroys my skin,
for underneath it, passion burns.
His fire burns up every nerve in my body.
So, you ask who I am? I am nothing but a name.
Everything else is Him.

JELALUDDIN RUMI, SUFI

The light of the Beloved rises
from the horizon of my heart,
drink from the cup,
you are the owners of sight.

MOULANA SHAH MAGHSOUD, SUFI

On this sacred ground
God has anointed me with grace,
and brought me face to face with the Beloved.

OLGA RASMUSSEN

Time allows the world to run on time . . .
but we are free to delight in the Beloved's brilliance.
My blows against the glass to break through to You
are weak and ineffective, but at least the glass mirrors
Your beautiful face.

I am still in time, but no longer subject to its oppression.
I simply let You do with me what You wish.
This marvelous universe and the sacred garden
which is this earth will both pass away when Your Gaze
breaks the mirror of my mind.

BULLEH SHAH, SUFI

I find the Beloved in the night, and my heart aches.
When sunrise comes, the lover wakes from his heartache.
Still, the lover wants no relief from the ache of separation—
for how else will he know of the Beloved's existence?

The experience of daylight is torture for the lover,
like a fish brought up from the water and tossed
onto the sand to die. The fish gasps for the sea
like the lover desires to breathe in the night that will
reveal its islands of stars,
and carry the lover to the far shore.

MIRABAI, VEDANTA (HINDU)

Fire is everywhere—all of creation is in flames.
"This is My passion," the Beloved said.

ABU-SAID ABIL-KHEIR, SUFI

Take all that I am—my mind, my heart,
my senses, my will and my thoughts.
All these—all that I am—I give to You.

VLADIMIR SOLOVYOV, RUSSIAN ORTHODOX

No longer does Janibai wish to stay
on the wheel of samsara,
but how will I burn off my remaining karma?
I leave it to You to provide me grist for the mill.
Grind me up. Pound me into powder.

JANABAI, VEDANTA (HINDU)

Was it my reason that led me to You?
I once thought so.
I even thought I felt your presence
and saw your perfect countenance.

But all this was imperfect knowledge.
That which I thought to be true was actually false.
Those who really see You cannot describe you.
Everything is turned upside down.
Night is day and day is night,
and virtue cannot be found anywhere.

The soul thinks what's false is true.
To truly find You, it is necessary
to lose all human powers.
We enter the darkness and
develop new eyes.
Then the soul finds
that which it was not even looking for.
Everything else is stripped away.

Cast oneself into the ocean and let it drown.
Then everything becomes new again.
How this happens I do not know.

JACOB DA TODI, ROMAN CATHOLIC

The Beloved gives itself to all lovers,
so that all lovers may become the Beloved.
This is absolute unity, beauty and love.
The lover's love becomes so intense that
it leaves no trace of itself, and only
the Beloved remains.

MEHER BABA, SUFI

Holding me in your loving arms, Beloved,

you have given me the greatest gift of all:

Yourself.

I sought nothingness, and in the seeking,

my heart was purified.

It rose to become one with You.

MARGUERITE PORETE, ROMAN CATHOLIC

As you came ever closer to me,

I thought of You so often

that I completely became

You.

Little by little You drew near,

and slowly but slowly I passed away.

JAVAD NURBAKHSH, SUFI

Give me all those things that are

difficult and austere, Beloved, so that

You may have all that is gentle and pleasing.

JOHN OF THE CROSS, ROMAN CATHOLIC

The Beloved asked what I needed.
I sought the truth and asked for compassion and wisdom.
These things I needed in order to become one with the Beloved.

RAM DASS, VEDANTA (HINDU)

"What did I give you that you should love Me?"
I replied: "Sorrows and pleasures.
I no longer see the difference between them."

RAMON LLULL, ROMAN CATHOLIC

I have cried many tears, and everyone knows this.
I gave You my body and mind a long time ago,
seeking refuge in You.
I see Your feet pass, even as I escape
from one life to another.
I am your virgin.

MIRABAI, VEDANTA (HINDU)

It takes no effort on our part
for Your love to reach us, Beloved.
You come like a bird that hangs into air motionless.
We live and move in the world of the Beloved—
one body and soul between us,
though we appear separate in form.

MECHTHILD OF MAGDEBURG, ROMAN CATHOLIC

Losing myself in concentration,
I thought my practice would quickly
lead me to You.
But I found, Instead, that only You
knew the ways to approach You.
But I can no longer live without you,
and you do not allow me to flee.
I have lost consciousness of myself.
I have died to self so that I may become Yours.
But how long must I wait, Beloved?
I am exhausted from being separated from You.
Banish me no more.

ABU 'I HUSYN AL-NURI, SUFI

I have looked for You from sunup to sundown.
I have reached out for You in every direction,
turning my face this way and that.
Now I am so thirsty that I must plead
for Your grace like a beggar.

Even the heavens are too small to hold you,
but perhaps you could carve out
a small niche in the cliffs for me.

SOLOMON 'IBIN-GABIROL, JEWISH

After the earth and humanity
have long disappeared;
after all the universes You created
have ceased to be—
You will be alone, holding all existence,
as potential, within Yourself.
There is no room for death here.
No atom can cease to be.
You are Being and Spirit,
and can never be destroyed.

EMILY BRONTË, ROMAN CATHOLIC

The Beloved tested his lover by asking
what difference there was between
His presence and lack of it.
The lover replied that it was the difference
between ignorance and forgetfulness
and knowledge and remembrance.

When your ego releases your heart,
then you will see the Beloved.
Just as you cannot see yourself except
in a mirror, gaze upon the Beloved—
who is your mirror.

JELALUDDIN RUMI, SUFI

I would give my soul to see Your face,
to gaze into Your blessed eyes.
I sacrifice myself for the sake of love
and cast myself into the flames of love's passion.
What sweet grace; I die so that I might live again.
For while you slay me, Lord, it is so that I may live in You.

RICHARD CRENSHAW, PROTESTANT

I am not the intellect or the ego or emotions.
I am not the sky nor the earth; neither rock or metals.
I am You, blessed spirit, I am You.
I was not born, nor will I die.
I have no father and mother.
I am You, blessed Spirit, I am You.

Beyond anything that can be imagined,
I am without form, but fill the limbs of all things.
Nothing can bind me, so I do not fear.
I am free forever, for I am You, blessed spirit,
I am You.

SHANKARA, VEDANTA (HINDU)

When Love flowed into my veins,
that which had been me flowed out.
Every limb and organ became the Beloved,
and occupied every space.
All that is left of me is a name.

ABU-SAID ABIL-KHEIR, SUFI

How can I love Him when I do not exist?
It is He who loves me. He exists, I do not.
Whatever He wills becomes my passion.
His fullness that sparked this life within me.
Now I carry His seed of steadfast Love.

MARGUERITE PORETE, ROMAN CATHOLIC

She came to me in royal blue today, my queen.
She stood before me and my heart was
filled with sweetness and light. But something
in the distance was burning to the ground.
I could almost smell the smoke.

VLADIMIR SOLOVYOV, RUSSIAN ORTHODOX

I was born already yours.

You made me, tolerated me, redeemed me.

You waited for me to come to You

and you called me Your own.

But what can I—a poor wretch—give to you?

You see me through your eyes of love

and mold me to your purpose, so that

I am yours alone—heart, body and soul.

Give me life or give me death.

Give me health or give me sickness.

Make me a pauper, or give me a fortune;

it makes no difference.

I am yours to do with as you wish.

But what can I give to You?

TERESA OF AVILA, ROMAN CATHOLIC

Even if I go blind I will still see You.
Even if I become deaf, I will hear You.
Take away my feet
and I will still make my way to You.
Take away my arms,
and I will still embrace You.
Make my heart stop,
and my mind will take up its beat.
Consume me with fire and every drop
of my blood will become ablaze.

RAINER MARIA RILKE

With gratitude, I am joyful to participate
in the sacred banquet.
My heart embraces Him who angels
praise without ceasing.

Your love sets our love on fire.
Our nourishment comes from contemplating You.
Your grace fills our every need.

CLARE OF ASSISI, ROMAN CATHOLIC

The light that comes with wisdom
turns time into a dream, and even
forces death to retreat.
The name of the eternal Beloved
hides within my heart,
yet I am a meek and timid lover.

VLADIMIR SOLOVYOV, RUSSIAN ORTHODOX

I put an end to knowledge and wisdom,
and let thinking disappear into the Great Void.
If I repent for all my wrongs,
how will my heart ever rest?
I go fishing in the one stream
and catch joy as if it were riches.
Letting go, there is nothing left to do but sing—
for my thoughts have drowned in the Great Void.

CHI K'ANG, TAOIST

ONENESS

Becoming What We Already Are

—◦◦◦—

In the beginning, there was no being and no non-being.
There was no air, no sky, no death, no immortality.
Darkness was hidden in the void, but what was hidden in it?
The One breathed, but nothing else existed.

Then the One forced itself into existence.
Desire entered the One and planted
the seeds of mind and matter.
A beam of light shot across the universe:
creation, fertility, energy and desire came into being.

Who can say where creation came from?
Or whether or not He produced it?
Only He knows.
Or perhaps He does not know.

FROM THE HYMN OF CREATION, THE VEDAS, VEDANTA (HINDU)

Once the One slept—
not knowing of Its own existence.
He was like an ocean with no shore,
where no wind or waves moved.
There were no stars, no sun, no earth.
There was nothing but Him,
but all things were in Him.
He slept, unformed and un-manifested.
He had knowledge of Himself,
but did not know that he knew.

But then came the desire to know who He was.
So He brought forth everything from nothing,
and caused Himself to exist.
He became rock, and thought that was who He was
for millions of years.
Then he thought he was vegetation, and lived as vegetation
for millions of years.
But He felt He was more than that, so he became all animals,
and lived as worms and snails and fishes
and birds and mammals for millions of years.
But still He thought He was more than that and so created man.
Now the One finally knew who He was,
because in man, He saw his own reflection.

FRANCIS BRABAZON, SUFI

God said, "Let it be," and it became.

The Un-manifest became manifest.

He gave life to the lifelessness, Created form out of formlessness.

Such a wonderful game He played with Himself.

So that His existence would be a secret, He hid behind a veil.

Then He lifted the veil to show that He exists in everyone.

What a wonderful game He plays.

BULLEH SHAH, SUFI

He is the form which is formless,

the body without a body,

the countenance that is invisible,

the name that cannot be spoken,

the mind which cannot be conceived of.

He is a fountain, for all things flow from Him.

He is the root of all that He planted,

the Light that enlightens the world,

the Love of those who love Him,

the fortune of those for whom he cares,

the wisdom of those to whom he has given wisdom,

the power of those to whom he has given power.

He gathers all things to Himself,

and all things gather in Him.

He is the revelation of all who seek,

the eye of all who see,

the breath of all who breathe,

the life of all who live,

the unity of All that is.

All things exist in Him,

and they are One.

THE TRIPARTITE TRACTATE, GNOSTIC-CHRISTIAN

In the beginning there was a beauty which
polished the mirror of creation.
It embraced every particle of a hundred thousand suns.
Yet there was no witness to this glory
until the eyes of humanity were opened.
Only then was He known.

ABDUL-QADER BEDIL, SUFI

Human existence begins with the belief
that we are separate,
then moves on to trying to find our way back
to the One of which we are not just a part,
but who, in fact, we are.

RAM DASS, VEDANTA (HINDU)

The human body is the same as the cosmic body.
The human mind is the same as the cosmic mind.
The microcosm is the same as the macrocosm.
In one atom exists the entire universe.

THE UPANISHADS, VEDANTA (HINDU)

What exists between
God and the soul?
Nothing.

MOTHER JULIAN OF NORWICH, ROMAN CATHOLIC

Who is it who loves and suffers?
It is He who is playing a game with Himself.
We suffer because we think ourselves
to be separate from Him.
But if we come to recognize the One
in all things and in all places,
pain and suffering will come to an end.

SRI ANANDAMAYI MA, VEDANTA (HINDU)

When He takes possession of the soul,
it is Love that eats His flesh and drinks His blood.
But it is also Love which devours the soul itself,
so that only He remains.

HADEWIJCH, ROMAN CATHOLIC

The Universe and I were born together.
All things are only One thing.

CHUANG TZU, TAOIST

We may know Him by many names,
but He is one and the same to all.

MAHATMA GANDHI

I am the highest and the lowest.
I am all that exists.

MOTHER JULIAN OF NORWICH, ROMAN CATHOLIC

When my body became You,
there was no one else to serve but You.
When my mind became You,
there was no one else I could call upon.
After my own consciousness was lost in You,
there was nothing else to know.
Losing myself in You,
"You" and "I" ceased to exist.

AKKA MAHADEVI, VEDANTA (HINDU)

—◦◦◦—

Walking upon my path, I found that my former friends
had become enemies.
But I received solace from the One True Friend.
When I realized Oneness, I became free of the many.
Now I am His and He is mine.

SARMAD, SUFI, JEWISH

—◦◦◦—

It is beyond human expression—
that I am rich, It is a marvel that cannot be expressed.
Although I have riches, it makes me needy like
one who imagines that he has nothing.
Even as I possess so much, I say,
"Who will give me?"
Even though I am in the midst
of abundant waters,
I say, "I am thirsty."
I see the One every day, yet say,
"Where will I find it?"
There is nothing to hold onto, the One within me—
that which is beyond the world and invisible.

SYMEON THE NEW THEOLOGIAN, EASTERN ORTHODOX

We will never find God until we learn
that He exists in every living being,
including ourselves.

SWAMI VIVEKANANDA, VEDANTA (HINDU)

I seek only One thing:
the All that exists in everything.
All things are born of the One.
All things flow from the One.
The One is not just in all things,
but above all things.
This God holds me within my own heart.

DAME CATHERINE GASCOIGNE, ROMAN CATHOLIC

All that is, is One Mind.
It is eternal and clear.
It embraces all realities—
both the visible and the invisible.

PADMASAMBHAVA, TIBETAN BUDDHIST

When the Many are reduced to One,
to what is the One reduced?

ZEN KOAN

When you were already One,
you became two.
Now what will you do?

JESUS, *THE GOSPEL OF THOMAS*

One master asked his teacher:
"Where can Tao be found?"
The teacher replied:
"Where *can't* Tao be found?"

CHAN BUDDHIST STORY

He is the knowledge, the knower,
and that which is known.
All things are united in Him,
and are imbued with His essence.
He is Being—
in which all things have their existence
and perfection.

MOSES CORDOVERO, FROM THE *KABALA*, JEWISH

Blessed are they who find the One
within their own being.

JESUS, *THE GOSPEL OF THOMAS*

Be joyful and behold the One in all things.

MOTHER JULIAN OF NORWICH, ROMAN CATHOLIC

Only that which is in you—
which is also in me—
can hear what I'm saying.

RAM DASS, VEDANTA (HINDU)

All that appears different in the world
is a matter of degree, not kind.
The secret is, all things are One.

SWAMI VIVEKANANDA, VEDANTA (HINDU)

Let your presence within me set me on fire,
so that I am transformed into You—
so that all separation between You and me
ceases in Your all consuming love.

THOMAS A' KEMPIS, ROMAN CATHOLIC

Once a person attains unity,
others can no longer relate to him.
He exists beyond both being and non-being.
While others still want to transcend ordinary life,
he just returns from the farthest shore
and sits down in coal and ashes.

TUNG-SHAN, CHAN BUDDHIST

I come from the One
who is beyond all distinctions.
Anyone who is solitary and united within himself
becomes full of light.
But anyone who is divided within himself
is filled with darkness.

JESUS, *THE GOSPEL OF THOMAS*

The nature of God is a circle of which the center is
everywhere and the circumference is nowhere.

PLOTINUS

It is a mystery how Your body possesses my mind,
and my soul becomes yours.
What I was, I no longer am.
You come, You go, but You have sown the seed
that will lead to glory long after this body turns to dust.

EDITH STEIN, ROMAN CATHOLIC

Break a stalk of bamboo in half
and make the top half male
and the bottom half female.
Rub them together like kindling
until they ignite.
Now, which part of the fire is male
and which is female?

DERVA DASIMAYYA, VEDANTA (HINDU)

After the birds have left for the day,
and the last cloud disappears,
the mountain and I sit together
until only the mountain remains.

LI PO, TAOIST

―₪₪₪―

I behold God with the same eye
with which he beholds me.

MEISTER ECKHART, ROMAN CATHOLIC

―₪₪₪―

God, the Father of everything, the invisible One,
cannot be penetrated or divided.
That which is above everything is
incorruptible, without limits, and eternal.
He is the pure Light into which
no one can look.
He is pure Mind.

THE APOCRYPHON OF JOHN, GNOSTIC-CHRISTIAN

You ask what Tao is,
but words cannot describe what It is.
You want further explanation?
This means This.

Li Tung Po, Taoist

There is no point in coming and going
like the waves of the ocean.
That which ebbs is the same as that which flows.
The people of the world and the heart of the Buddha;
what difference is there?

Hsu Yun, Chan Buddhist

I sang with You during the day,
and we slept together at night.
But I am confused;
I thought I was I,
but it was You.

Jelaluddin Rumi, Sufi

Humanity is like coverings for pillows.
Some are one color, some are another.
Still, they are all made from the same material.
It is the same with humanity.
One man may be handsome and another not.
One may be sinful, while another is pure.
But the same spirit of the One dwells within them all.

SRI RAMAKRISHNA, VEDANTA (HINDU)

Our true home of majesty lies beyond duality.

JELALUDDIN RUMI, SUFI

The wise man faithfully remains with the One
and becomes an example for all to see.
He does not stand out so he is a light for all.
He thinks nothing of himself,
so others honor him.

THE TAO TE CHING, TAOIST

There is nowhere you can go where I am not.

I am in you and you are in Me.

My seed is in everything.

When you gather the harvest, you gather Me.

FRAGMENT FROM THE LOST *GOSPEL OF EVE*, GNOSTIC-CHRISTIAN

We are two souls in one body.

It is You that I love in myself.

See me and you see Him.

See Him and you see everyone.

MANSUR AL-HALLAJ, SUFI

We dwell in your heart, and You dwell in ours.

We come forth from You like the petals of a flower.

You plant the seed in us so that we may grow

and bear fruit in Your garden—

so that we may return the fruit to You.

The One dwells like a fish in the sea

and the sea in the fish.

CATHERINE OF SIENA, ROMAN CATHOLIC

No one can know the truth if they are concerned
with their wives and husbands,
mothers and fathers, sisters and brothers.
The Self is without gender.
It is everyone's father, mother, child, friend and foe.
The One is in all. Only the Self exists.

SWAMI VIVEKANANDA, VEDANTA (HINDU)

Studying Buddha nature is the same as studying yourself.
Studying yourself requires forgetting yourself.
To become enlightened is to become free—
which means being free of one's own mind and body
as well as the minds and bodies of others.
Once achieved, even this enlightenment disappears,
and cannot be found anywhere even though it exists forever.

DOGEN, ZEN BUDDHIST

You are the absolute Light
which can see with pure eyes
beyond the haze of our limitations.
Your light is hidden everywhere in the world,
and the world reveals Your beauty.

Your gift to me was to become one with You.
It is Your blood that runs through my veins.
I have become one with Your pure body—
transparent, holy and filled with light.

SYMEON THE NEW THEOLOGIAN, EASTERN ORTHODOX

The beginning of things
is the same as the end of things.
Creation is no different than destruction.
All things are one and the same in the Tao.

CHUANG TZU, TAOIST

Joyfulness comes in realizing that our soul
and the soul of the entire world
are one and the same.
Such recognition is love supreme.

RABINDRANATH TAGORE, VEDANTA (HINDU)

I and the Father are One.

JESUS, THE GOSPEL OF JOHN

The many do not exist; there is only the One.
At-one-ment is the realization that duality is an illusion.

PADMASAMBHAVA, TIBETAN BUDDHIST

Do all the normal things in life.
Come and go, look, listen, smell, touch, taste.
Pass your time in simple conversation,
but let the mind not stray from oneness.

SARAHA, BUDDHIST

Passing over all multitude of things,
and serving Me with resolute devotion,
such a person becomes ready to attain
oneness with the Supreme.

THE BHAGAVAD GITA, VEDANTA (HINDU)

Once my body became Yours,
who else could I serve?
Once my mind became Yours,
who else could I appeal to?
After my perception became Yours,
who else could I know?
Because of You, I have forgotten You.

AKKA MAHADEVI, VEDANTA (HINDU)

Whether there be joy or sorrow, happiness or anger,
all emotions cease when one realizes that all of creation
is One.
United in One, the physical body becomes
nothing more than the dust of the earth.

CHUANG TZU, TAOIST

Where can I find you Lord?
Your place is grand and undisclosed.
And where can I find You not?
Your glory is everywhere upon the earth.

JUDAH HALEVI, JEWISH

All things are Brahman—
that from which all things originate,
and that into which all things will dissolve.

THE CHANDOGYA UPANISHAD, VEDANTA (HINDU)

He has no form and no qualities,
and yet He takes on form and qualities.
He plays this illusory game
of hide and seek with Himself alone.
His cosmic game is endless,
having no beginning and no end.
He is the whole and He is the part—
such is His perfection.

SRI ANANDAMAYI, VEDANTA (HINDU)

In the beginning was the Word,
and the Word was with God,
and the Word *was* God.

THE GOSPEL OF JOHN

He is always with them,
and they are never separated
even for an instant.
If only they knew.

MANSUR AL HALLAJ, SUFI

Where is God? Where is He not?
God penetrates all things like a string
running through a garland of flowers.
He is hidden as fire in wood,
scent in flowers, salt in seawater.
As restless rivers rush ever onward
to rejoin the sea, so we remain restive
until we become one with Him.
God is our source and our destination.

SWAMI SIVANANDA, VEDANTA (HINDU)

Nature could not exist
if it were not filled with God.
Nature is mystical. It seeks the One.

MEISTER ECKHART, ROMAN CATHOLIC

The animating principle of all things is the Self,
the One within many.
The wise see His existence inside themselves
and attain to eternal bliss.

THE KATHA UPANISHAD, VEDANTA (HINDU)

Your love shines through my eyes,
for you fill me with Yourself.

JELALUDDIN RUMI, SUFI

Where is Tao?

If you look for it, you won't see it.
It comes in and goes out,
but doesn't use doors.
It is the very smallest of all things,
yet it is everywhere.
If you fail to recognize it,
you will meet it without knowing.

HAN-SHAN, TAOIST, CHAN BUDDHIST

If you seek God, become molten
and let yourself melt away.
Take the path of understanding
and give yourself totally to the journey.
Where there was nothing, find Being.
Get drunk on the wine of God.

HAKIM ABU-AL-MAJD, SUFI

If one does not recognize God,
the barrier lies within his own mind.
For God is all things, and has become
all things within the individual.

MEISTER ECKHART, ROMAN CATHOLIC

That which dwells in all creatures—the Self—
is that which controls the universe.
He is manifest in all objects and creatures,
and those who find it within themselves have eternal Bliss.

THE KATHA UPANISHAD, VEDANTA (HINDU)

Duality proceeds from the One,
but let go of clinging even to this One.
When the mind is fully stable,
no mind, no blame, no phenomena remain.
The observer vanishes along with the object of observation.
Both disappear into oblivion since that which is observed exists
only in the mind of the observer.
When the observer and that which is observed disappear,
duality ceases.

SENG-TS'AN, CHAN BUDDHIST

I cannot speak of the great mystery within.

Words fail to describe it.

Neither can I hold onto the One which exists beyond that.

Being invisible, having no form, not being mixed with anything else,

such reality is ineffable.

I have found myself moving within this Totality

like a candle's flame lighting another candle.

When this light fills every part of us,

manifesting reality, all that was hurtful, dark, full of shame

is transformed by Him.

SYMEON THE NEW THEOLOGIAN,
EASTERN ORTHODOX

Men will live and wander within creation

from the beginning of creation until the end.

It is possible for him to align his nature with the One.

CHUANG TZU, TAOIST

Having examined all religions, I have realized
that God is the Whole and I am His part.
We are One.
He manifests Himself in never-ending forms
to fulfill the desires of those devoted to Him.
But He, Himself, is formless.
He cannot be divided because
He is the Absolute.

SRI RAMAKRISHNA, VEDANTA (HINDU)

I am not a distant God.
I dwell within you as a brother and a friend.
You, in turn, dwell within Me.
Behold. We are One!

WILLIAM BLAKE

I am intoxicated with my oneness with You.
There is nothing else I need, want or care about.

JELALUDDIN RUMI, SUFI

You have no beginning or end,

yet have become He who preserves and protects us.

You are the All, beyond comparison, beyond limits,

without visual essence, without attributes, beyond division,

beyond description, beyond understanding.

You are imperishable.

You may only be seen by those with spiritual eyes,

even though you are everywhere and within everything—

both manifest and un-manifest simultaneously.

No one can see you without divine eyesight,

even though You are everywhere and in everything.

You are both manifest and un-manifest.

You are infinite power and bliss.

You are the Knower and that which is known.

You are Truth, Bliss, Love.

You are beyond the beyond.

MEHER BABA, SUFI

Suddenly,
like an explosive crack across the universe,
there is clear understanding.
It is that which consumed the Buddhas
and ancestors before you.
Follow no one; seek union.

DOGEN, ZEN BUDDHIST

The only thing that God expects from you
is that you leave yourself behind and realize
that you are made of Him.

MEISTER ECKHART, ROMAN CATHOLIC

Understanding at last.
Suddenly the ocean is dried out
and there is nothing to block the view.
Nothing else exists.

JOHO, ZEN BUDDHIST

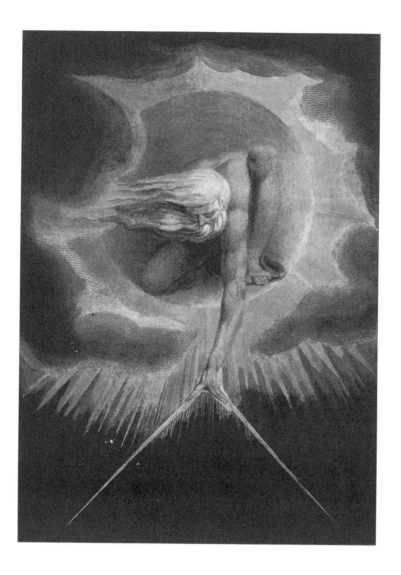

Wherever I wander, there is only You.
Whatever I think about, it is You.
Everywhere, there is only You.
In the sky, upon the earth,
above us and below us,
in the beginning and at the end,
there is only You!

LEVI YITZCHAK, JEWISH

Free will does not exist,
since all things are subject to cause and effect.
Yet there is something behind the will that is free.

SWAMI VIVEKANANDA, VEDANTA (HINDU)

Beyond and within all existence is the One.

JELALUDDIN RUMI, SUFI

A certain man rejected
all other emanations of God but Shiva—
even though Shiva, himself, rebuked
the man for his narrow-mindedness.

To make his point, Shiva took on the
appearance of Hari-har.
Half of him was Shiva
and half of him was Vishnu.
It made no difference.
The man refused to worship
the half that was Vishnu.

Shiva said to the man,
"You are an impossible dogmatist.
Even by taking on a dual aspect
I could not convince you that all gods
and goddesses are just aspects of the
One, Absolute, Brahman."

SRI RAMAKRISHNA, VEDANTA (HINDU)

I see His hand move my hand,
It is He who speaks in my voice.
As I go from room to room,
I find no one there but Him.

JELALUDDIN RUMI, SUFI

How can You be the source of water as well as the fire?
How do You make us One with You?

SYMEON THE NEW THEOLOGIAN, EASTERN ORTHODOX

We may appear separate, but we are one.
He never leaves me.
We go everywhere together—
like the flower and its fragrance.

SARMAD, SUFI

As the sea of knowing-mind runs dry,
shining jewels appear on their own.
Watching the cosmos reduced to dust,
I see a moon hanging all alone.
I cast a net into space and caught
dragon and phoenix.
I walk through the cosmos alone,
linking together the past and its people.

HSU YUN, CHAN BUDDHIST

When self-love ceases,
and love of goodness takes its place,
then you will be One with the Beloved.
Loving Him, He must also love you.
That love draws you to Him and Him to You.
And the two become One.
In such union there is no division.

JACOPONE DA TODI, ROMAN CATHOLIC

Phenomena are really nothing more
than the veils in which God cloaks Himself.
Were it not for your estrangement,
you would look upon Him face to face.

AL-GHAZZOLI, SUFI

The divine is like a wheel or a circle
that cannot be grasped by the human mind.
And as a circle, it has no beginning or end.

HILDEGARD OF BINGEN, ROMAN CATHOLIC

Throughout eternity, that which we call Mind
has never been born and has never died.
Changeless, it has no past or future.
It is not subject to cause and effect.
It is not good or evil, true or false, male or female.
Mind is no one's property and it does not seek liberation.
It is formless and hard to perceive since it is not subject to the senses.
Many are those who seek It,
yet they do not realize that it already lies
within themselves.
It is what gives them life.

BODHIDHARMA, ZEN BUDDHIST

I will know that I am free from bondage
on the day when I can finally see God
in every human being, and every being
as the temple of God,
When I stand in reverence of the One in all,
all else will vanish and I will be free.

SWAMI VIVEKANANDA, VEDANTA (HINDU)

—⟨∿⟩—

God is in you and God is in me.
He is hidden in all things, so let go
of your pride and vanity and seek
Him within yourself.

KABIR, SUFI

—⟨∿⟩—

I am the reflection of you, Lord.

MECHTHILD OF MAGDEBURG, ROMAN CATHOLIC

—⟨∿⟩—

That which is truly real lies
within everyone in the world.

DOGEN, ZEN BUDDHIST

Men and women blush should their nakedness be revealed.
But the entire world is the eye of God, and it sees everything
everywhere.
What is there to hide?

ARKA MAHADEVI, VEDANTA (HINDU)

Everything is God—the pot, the pan, the comb,
the stick, the string of a bow.
Gods are so numerous there is no room left
to set down one's foot.
Yet God is One, and the One is the only God.

BASAVA, VEDANTA (HINDU)

What is there between you and God?
Nothing.

NIFFARI, SUFI

Universal form is like crystal.
Its perception changes according to circumstances.

SARYAJNAMITA, TANTRIC BUDDHIST

You assume all shapes, ride the winds
and make Your way through storms.
The sea itself becomes Your road.
Your emissaries take every form and
complete every mission with fear and
trembling, terror and awe—
then, at long last, open to You.

YANNI, JEWISH

You will only be fully fit to serve others
when you no longer see the difference
between yourself and others.
Winning success in serving others you will
meet Me and in finding Me you will reach
Buddhahood.

MILAREPA, TIBETAN BUDDHIST

When I thought of the greatness
of what was human,
I found myself in the divine.

JUAN RAMON JIMENEZ

Teach me to worship you in all that exists.
Fill the stillness of my soul and make me
aware of Your Presence in me and around me.

PARAMAHANSA YOGANANDA, VEDANTA (HINDU)

Finally have I realized that I am what I have been seeking.
I have found bliss is the realm beyond the knower and the known.
Mind, form, will, thought—all have ceased.
The goal has been reached and the truth has been revealed.
I am the way—the soul of God. My cosmic play has ended.

SRI CHINMOY, VEDANTA (HINDU)

I am far too weak and feeble to express
the mysteries of the Blessed.
But I am His image and temple.

THOMAS TRAHERNE

When quitting time, I am Myself eternity.
I shall be one with God, God shall be one with me.

ANGELUS SILESIUS, ROMAN CATHOLIC

The nighttime is empty—
nothing from the mountains to the sea.
But I am not alone, for You rock me.
The sky is deserted.
Even the moon falls into the sea.
But I am not alone, for You hold me.
The world itself is deserted,
all creatures are sad to see.
But I am not alone, for You hug me.

GABRIELA MISTRAL

—⁓—

I am you and you are me.
We exist interdependently.
As we work on ourselves personally,
others benefit at the same time.

THICH NHAT HANH, ZEN BUDDHIST

—⁓—

You wake my heart, and this light within me has been lit by You.
Now I know that You and I are not separate.

RABINDRANATH TAGORE, VEDANTA (HINDU)

When you perceive that the two are One,
that the outer is the same as the inner,
that which is above is the same as that which is below,
that the male and the female are one and the same—
then you will enter the kingdom of God.

JESUS, *THE GOSPEL OF THOMAS*

No longer am I trapped by the illusion that my body
is anything more than the play of the universe.
I have escaped from this illusion.
That which is within is the same as that which is without.
That which is infinite is the same as that which is finite.
Seeing all things anew, I have become drunk with the
light of God that fills the universe.
Life and death no longer have any hold on me.

KABIR, SUFI

I saw the One before me in the desert.
In the vastness there was only You.
Now these roses in my soul will never wither,
no matter the vagaries of life.

VLADIMIR SOLOVYOV, RUSSIAN ORTHODOX

It is a secret that every illumined being is aware of,
and this secret is hidden even from the heavens.
The mullah thinks that Ahmad went to heaven.
Sarmad says that heaven was already inside Ahmad.

SARMAD, SUFI, JEWISH

Some say that there is a darkness in God,
but perhaps what appears to be dim is due
to not seeing clearly.
I long for this dark night so that I might live in Him.

HENRY VAUGHN

I have tried to be near to You,
calling out for you with my voice.
But when I went out to look for You,
I saw You coming to me.

JUDAH HALEVI, JEWISH

As I walk I know that it is You who is walking,
even if I don't see You.
I try to visit You, but sometimes I forget You exist.
I talk, but the One remains silent.
This One is forgiving, even when I am not.
This One goes walking while I remain inside.
This One will remain standing when I die.

JUAN RAMON JIMENEZ

Our lives are in God, as God is within us.
He nurtures all creatures, and even though
His splendor is often hidden from us,
it abides in all life.
God is the life of all that exists.

HILDEGARD OF BINGEN, ROMAN CATHOLIC

You are in me as water is mingled with wine.

There is nothing that happens to You

that doesn't also happen to me.

You and I are One soul.

MANSUR AL-HALLAJ, SUFI

Two are not without God,

but the one who is unified within himself *is* God.

With such vision I am found everywhere—

beneath a stone, even within a piece of wood.

JESUS, FRAGMENT OF A LOST GOSPEL

A beggar with bowl in hand knocks on his own door

because he has forgotten who he really is.

This is an illness that my teacher has cured me of:

God asking God for alms.

KABIR, SUFI

I am the frog that swims happily in the pond.
But I am also the snake that feeds on the frog.

THICH NHAT HANH, ZEN BUDDHIST

Only the One who manifests form
out of formlessness is able to win my heart.
He laughs at the world, which is Himself.

JELALUDDIN RUMI, SUFI

I praised You during the day
and stayed with You at night.
I always thought it was me,
but I was You all along.

JELALUDDIN RUMI, SUFI

What is there to argue about?
Both Hindus and Muslims are Him.
Eliminate duality.
Think of everyone as good.
Do not recognize the existence of thieves.
He resides in everyone,
though He tricks us by putting on masks.

BULLEH SHAH, SUFI

He painted all the worlds with colors,
but the colors are only fantasy.
The colors, "I" and "you," cannot be purchased.
Better to take on His colorlessness.

AYAN AL-QOZAT HAMADANI, SUFI

Put yourself into His arms
and do not recognize
any difference between the worlds.

SARMAD, SUFI

When I am near to your Heart,
I forget everything else.
I am no longer in the grip of fear.
Let me have a place in Your heart.
Become One in me.

THÉRÈSE OF LISIEUX, ROMAN CATHOLIC

God leaned over me and
whispered sweet words in my ear.
He embraced me like the sea embraces
the stream that rushes to her.
When I found myself down in the valley,
God was also there.

KAHLIL GIBRAN

It is simple to mistake the One for the other,
and the other for the One, for they are both one image.

HEKHALOT HYMN, JEWISH

You flow through us as tears flow from our eyes.
You dwell in our innermost regions:
our hearts and souls.
Nothing that has motion and nothing
that rests is not filled with You.

MANSUR AL-HALLAJ, SUFI

The circle of the world embraces all things.

HADEWIJCH, ROMAN CATHOLIC

If we were worthy enough we would hear
the grass singing to God—
a song without motive or expectation of reward.
The best place to meditate is where things grow,
for there we can better compose our thoughts in God's presence.
Go to the grassy field. It will awaken your heart.

NACHMAN OF BRATZLAV, JEWISH

You are only the manifestation
of the You which is un-manifest.

ABU-SAID ABIL-KHEIR, SUFI

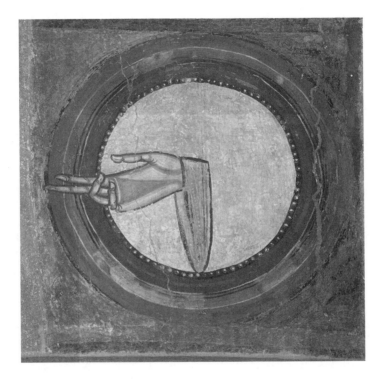

THE MYSTIC

—◦◦◦—

The mystic is someone who disappears
into what is truly real.

BINAVI BADAKHSHANI, SUFI

—◦◦◦—

Go into your chamber, shut the door,
and pray to your Father who is in secret,
so that He will reward you openly.

Seek and you shall find.
Knock and the door will be opened to you.

JESUS

Keep on knocking until the joy inside
opens a window.
Look to see who's there.

JELALUDDIN RUMI, SUFI

That which you are looking for,
is what is looking.

FRANCIS OF ASSISI, ROMAN CATHOLIC

Others have locked their doors
so that lovers can be alone
with each other.
I am alone with You.

RABI'A AL-ADAWIYYA, SUFI

Whether we know it or not, every individual is evolving.
From the outside it might appear that we are not moving,
but something within us is awake.
That something will eventually lead us
back to the truth of our real nature.

JELALUDDIN RUMI, SUFI

If the doors of perception were cleansed,
everything would appear to man as it is: infinite.

WILLIAM BLAKE

Look within your own heart for what you seek.

KABIR, SUFI

Humanity has been deluded into believing
that I am here and you are there—
when nothing exists between us.

YASUTANI ROSHI, ZEN BUDDHIST

Tao is an empty vessel,
yet you can draw from it endlessly.

THE TAO TE CHING, TAOIST

He who has eyes to see, let him see.

JESUS

The whole of life lies in the verb, "seeing."

PIERRE TEILHARD DE CHARDIN, ROMAN CATHOLIC

I sell mirrors to blind people.

KABIR, SUFI

When Reality appears, ignorance is abolished.
But as long as our perception is false,
we are distracted by things that make us suffer.
When our vision is corrected, suffering ends.

SHANKARA, VEDANTA (HINDU)

Don't bother analyzing yourself.
Just see who you really are.

YAGASWAMI, VEDANTA (HINDU)

If what you seek does not exist in any place,
what is the point of your pilgrimage?
If you wish to find your Self, the journey is
all about polishing the mirror of your heart.

HAKIM ABU-AL-MAJD, SUFI

If you are irritated by every rub,
how will your mirror be polished?

JELALUDDIN RUMI, SUFI

My heart's mirror was polished by love,
and then I began to understand the mysteries.
I rose out of my inner darkness and became
the Light for all to see.
Some say the path is difficult,
but for me it went so easily.

SHARIB NAWAZ, SUFI

Let yourself have a free mind,

owe no one,

enjoy what you have received,

and do not judge yourselves as above,

below or even equal to others.

THE BUDDHA

———❧❧———

Belief brings me only to your door.

I must disappear into Your mystery

before I can come in.

HAKIM SANI, SUFI

———❧❧———

The kingdom of God is within you.

JESUS

You say you want to dwell in the mountains, my friend?
Then there is no need to travel to India to find a mountain.
I've got a thousand peaks to choose from right here by this lake.
The grass is fragrant enough and the clouds are white enough
to hold me here. What holds you there in the world?

CHIO JAN, TAOIST

Thinking gives off smoke to prove the existence of fire.
A mystic sits inside the burning.
There are wonderful shapes in rising smoke
that imagination loves to watch. But it's a mistake
to leave the fire for that filmy sight.
Stay here at the flame's core.

JELALUDDIN RUMI, SUFI

No one who puts his hand to the plow,
and looks back, is ready for the kingdom of God.

JESUS

Our path to God requires that we must
give up everything else in life.
One must empty themselves entirely,
remaining in the dark about other creatures.
True understanding, love and joy cannot
be based on the senses.
It must be based on God alone—
the very thing that cannot be seen,
sensed or understood.

JOHN OF THE CROSS, ROMAN CATHOLIC

Nothing belongs to me except Krishna.
I have searched the world, and find nothing else worthy of love.
This makes me an outcast from my family.
I am in exile and spend my time, instead, in the presence of holy men.
Only in their company do I feel comfortable.

MIRABAI, VEDANTA (HINDU)

Freedom is attained one step at a time.
But if you want joy, renounce the world now.
Control the senses, and stop desiring things.
Letting go of things is the path of the ascetic.
To be attached to anything results in delusion.
On this path, even the body is burdensome,
so why take more baggage?

Your reward will come when you cease maintaining
the illusion of "I" and "mine."
Only sorrow can come from clinging to likes and dislikes.
Those who renounce everything will find salvation.
All others will remain in delusion.

TIRUVALLUVAR, VEDANTA (HINDU)

Let go of everything that ties you down—
whether it be gold or love or hate.
These things bind you.
Let go of them and become free.

SWAMI VIVEKANANDA, VEDANTA (HINDU)

Do not lay up treasures on earth,

where moth and rust consume

and thieves break in and steal,

but lay up treasure in heaven,

for where your treasure is,

there is your heart also.

No one can serve two masters,

for either you will hate the one and love the other,

or serve the one and despise the other.

You cannot serve both God and money.

Seek what is great and the little things

will be added to you.

Take no gold nor silver, nor copper in your belts,

no bag for your journey, not even two tunics,

nor sandals, nor a staff.

Go and sell all that you have and

give the money to the poor;

then you will have riches in heaven.

For the pleasures of this world are false,

and gold and silver have no substance.

Beware of a desire for things, for life
does not equal an abundance of possessions.

Those who love life will lose it. Those who hate life
in this world will preserve it in eternity.

Those who forsake family and possessions,
and willingly take up their cross and follow me,
will receive everything I have promised.
And I will reveal to him the hidden mysteries.

JESUS, FROM THE GOSPELS
OF MATTHEW, MARK, LUKE, JOHN, THOMAS
AND *DIALOGUE OF THE SAVIOR*

You say you seek freedom?
You cannot find it in the world.
Neither will you find it in books or temples.
The only one who binds you is you, yourself.
You drag yourself around as if a rope was tied to your neck.
Stop complaining and let go of the rope.

SWAMI VIVEKANANDA, VEDANTA (HINDU)

It is lust for things that puts humanity
in chains and holds it in bondage.
This will be the case as long they
seek those things that pass away.

JESUS, *THE BOOK OF THOMAS THE CONTENDER*, GNOSTIC-CHRISTIAN

Become passers-by.

JESUS, *THE GOSPEL OF THOMAS*

In order to reach union with the Divine
it is necessary to leave the intellect behind.
One must let go of things and empty oneself
of everything in order to make room for
the flood of divine illumination.

JOHN OF THE CROSS, ROMAN CATHOLIC

The mind has no substance in itself,

but is like a reflection in a mirror.

Once clear sight comes,

all that seems separate in the world

is recognized to be One.

The will—the ego—must die,

and once it is dead,

one will have peace of mind.

P'ANG YUN, ZEN BUDDHIST

I have burned down my house.

I hold a torch in my hand and will burn down

anyone's house who wants to follow me.

KABIR, SUFI

I have cast fire on the earth and, look,

I am guarding it until it blazes.

JESUS, *THE GOSPEL OF THOMAS*

The pain of separation from God
is felt equally by a monk with his beads
and a drunk in a tavern.
This is an open wound that will
ultimately guide you to your heart of hearts.

ABU-SAID ABIL-KHEIR, SUFI

God is hidden in the here and now.
The more you seek him,
the more He will reveal Himself to you.

ANGELUS SILESIUS, ROMAN CATHOLIC

I cast off my clothes, my shame and my pride for all to see.
I have become nothing but a whore for God.
Jani says, "Lord I have become a slut in order to
reach where you are."

JANABAI, VEDANTA (HINDU)

I thought that no beloved would ever appear for me in this world.

I could not see the roses for the thorns.

But then the rose garden appeared and no thorns remain.

I went about always dissatisfied, but none of that remains.

What remains is the One.

I used to have high regard for religion and custom,

but now, even religion does not exist for me.

NIYAZI MISRI, SUFI

You have built Your temple in my soul.

When I act, the actions are Your actions.

You have made a home in my body.

Even my senses experience You.

Sleeping, I meditate on You,

and every word I utter

is a prayer to You.

My life is no longer anything

but the worship of You.

SHANKARA, VEDANTA (HINDU)

I have been through the universe and have seen His light reflected everywhere. Those who return from the Light of His presence are incapable of writing about such glory. Intellect fails us more and more the closer we come to the goal. Even memory cannot recall what the soul now knows.

DANTE ALIGHIERI, ROMAN CATHOLIC

If we read descriptions of mystical experiences we find that all of them have to do with "spiritual poverty." Those who are mystics counsel that the practitioner abandons ownership of everything, even oneself, even one's own consciousness.

The mystic abandons proprietorship of both the external world of nature and the internal world of his own experience. It then becomes clear that we have never owned anything in life, even our own soul. As St. Paul said, "I had nothing, but possessed all things."

ALAN WATTS, ZEN BUDDHIST

Let Your Presence wholly inflame me, consume
and transform me into Yourself.

THOMAS A' KEMPIS, ROMAN CATHOLIC

I no longer have a place.
There is no trace of me remaining.
No longer having body and soul,
I dwell in the Soul of souls.
I am no longer conscious of duality.
I live in two worlds,
but they have become one and the same.

JELALUDDIN RUMI, SUFI

Meditate, live purely, be quiet.
Do your work with mastery.

THE BUDDHA

There is nothing for me to fear in a universe
that belongs to my Mother.
Living on Her estate is easy, and I experience
nothing but bliss.
I live here within the garden of oneness
without paying rent, and my residence here
can never be auctioned off because there are
no owners and nothing to own.
Lord Shiva manages Mother's holdings,
transcending all transactions.
There is no disharmony or injustice in this place
because nothing is separate.
Mother does not impose a tax upon me,
and my only obligation is to be a good steward
by always remembering Her.
I have but one desire:
to give away this pure love to all beings.

RAMPRASAD SEN, VEDANTA (HINDU)

In happiness I wander these mountains alone.

All I understand is joy.

I walk along until the water ends

and then sit awhile to watch the clouds.

Should I happen to meet an old woodworker,

we may talk and laugh awhile,

getting totally lost to time.

WANG WEI, CHAN BUDDHIST, TAOIST

I pay no attention to words or realities outside myself—

but only to that which comes directly from my heart.

Words have no substance or final cause in themselves.

The substance is in the heart, which is the interpretation of the words.

To dwell on words is to dwell on superficialities.

I want to set the heart on fire with love,

and I want to *be* the fire—

consuming all thoughts and expressions.

JELALUDDIN RUMI, SUFI

The truth is simply this:
there is no difference between saints and ordinary people.
There is no point in considering differences.
It is like asking for string when you already have a good strong rope.
Each dharma is known in the heart.
Once you understand the design of the illusory world,
you will have all you need to understand the ways
of life and death.

SU YUN, CHAN BUDDHIST

The goal of all life is to return to the Source.
God is our source and God is our destination.

SWAMI SIVANANDA, VEDANTA (HINDU)

By awakening to My words completely
you have become one with Me.
Now you are drunk just from My gaze.
I pour My wine eternally, and the one
who drinks is never filled up.
His inner heart is perpetually intoxicated.

QUSHAYRI, SUFI

To understand our self-nature, as well as the self-nature of humanity, we should focus on what has beauty and dignity among human kind. Doing so will rid you of a fearful mind, and change it into a spiritual warrior's mind. Warrior's mind is always young and full of confidence. It allows you to expand into space and take in that which has no beginning and no end.

CHOGYAM TRUNGPA RIMPOCHE, TIBETAN BUDDHIST

My soul was from the beginning.
It resided in Me as hidden treasure.
I created it from nothing, and in the end
it will return to Me.
You who are conscious of Me are neither
male nor female.
Fail Me not; take your rightful place in My heart.

RAMANA MAHARSHI, VEDANTA (HINDU)

By contemplating one's original Mind,
all things here below can be understood.
When understood, all illusory thoughts
of separation will dissolve by themselves.

MILAREPA, TIBETAN BUDDHIST

The Divine Name is nectar to be sipped.
Remove yourself from the company of ignorant
people and surround yourself with those who are righteous.
Listen for talk about God.
Rid your mind of all anger, greed and attachment.
Let yourself be absorbed into the divine.

MIRABAI, VEDANTA (HINDU)

My torment is that I do not recognize the torment.
You are as close to me as You are far away.
When will I find respite from this ordeal?

QUSHAYRI, SUFI

That which you seek is already here,
but you do not recognize it.

JESUS, *THE GOSPEL OF THOMAS*

Mind is everywhere,
but only those who know themselves
can recognize it.
Those who are bound by desires,
who have no self-control,
who hold incorrect beliefs
and follow the wrong practices,
only increase the ties that bind them.

PADMASAMBHAVA, TIBETAN BUDDHIST

Others may judge him crazy
because he wanders around alone,
and has no desire for those things they do.
But the Self within him is completely satisfied,
and he finds satisfaction everywhere he goes.

SHANKARA, VEDANTA (HINDU)

If you want to get at the kernel of something,
you must first break the shell.
Only then can you enjoy its true benefits.
Symbols of reality are not the same as reality itself,
so they must be destroyed.
Then you will come closer and closer
to what truly is.
When you finally reach the One,
there your soul must remain.

MEISTER ECKHART, ROMAN CATHOLIC

I have become so vast in infinity
that I no longer have any interest in mundane things.
I have grasped for and held the Uncreated,
and it undid me completely.
It opened me up so wide that all else is too restricted.
Those of you who have reached this place know it well.

HADEWIJCH, ROMAN CATHOLIC

The lamp of the body is the mind.
As long as you have harmony within yourself,
your bodies will be filled with light.
But if there is darkness in your heart,
the enlightenment you seek will not manifest.

JESUS, *THE BOOK OF THOMAS THE CONTENDER*, GNOSTIC-CHRISTIAN

You have filled us with such blessedness
from Your holy mind that our souls dwell
in You like salt in the sea.

CATHERINE OF SIENA, ROMAN CATHOLIC

You conquer all things when you discover the Self within you.
Then the law of Karma ceases to have power over you.
Being in a body is like wearing chains,
but beyond the body and beyond the individual ego
lies freedom.
When you come to know the Self within you,
then you are set free from bondage.

SWAMI VIVEKANANDA, VEDANTA (HINDU)

Mistaking the unreal for the real guarantees rebirth.

Wisdom is seeing the Reality that lies behind all appearances.

Those who do so will not come back here again.

When clinging, lust, anger and delusion cease, so does sorrow.

TIRUVALLUVAR, VEDANTA (HINDU)

Giving up one thing after another eventually frees us of pain.

The sooner we renounce all things, the sooner joy will enter us.

Do not be attached to those things recognized by the five senses.

Let go of all attachments at once.

Happiness awaits the ascetic.

FENG KAN, ZEN BUDDHIST

God pursues me. For while I long for rest,

He encourages me to reach Him by becoming a visionary.

RABBI ABRAHAM JOSHUA HESCHEL, JEWISH

All of God's creatures were created
to follow their own true natures.
My nature is to live in oneness with Him.

MECHTHILD OF MAGDEBURG, ROMAN CATHOLIC

It doesn't matter how many holy words one reads or hears,
if a person does not act on them, the teachings are worthless.

THE BUDDHA

All creatures in this created order
follow the laws of their own nature.
They are compelled to seek their place
in relationship to the Ground of Being,
and reach their ultimate home by
following their own instinct.

DANTE ALIGHIERI, ROMAN CATHOLIC

Let us be led out of ignorance and into the Light.
Let us climb to the highest peak of sacred mystic
scripture where God's mysteries are made plain.
The Word is absolute and unchanging.
It shines brightly in the darkest places.
Its light fills our blind minds with
beauty beyond imagining.

DIONYSIUS THE AREOPAGITE, EASTERN ORTHODOX

Do only what you do not regret.

THE BUDDHA

Do not do what you hate.

JESUS, *THE GOSPEL OF THOMAS*

Unless you live in solitude, you won't reach the truth.
Unless you let go of your ego-self, you won't realize your own value.
Unless you sacrifice everything for the Beloved's sake,
you will not find ultimate freedom from suffering.

ABU-SAID ABIL-KHEIR, SUFI

The path to wholeness can't be found by running
away from the things of the world and becoming solitary.
One must nurture inner solitude in all stations
and circumstances in life.

MEISTER ECKHART, ROMAN CATHOLIC

Because I have tasted of something above the world of the senses,
I have dedicated my life to gaining that which lies
beyond physical pleasure.

JOHN OF THE CROSS, ROMAN CATHOLIC

My path to You is rough and filled with potholes.
One moment, I think only of You;
the next, I eat and drink and forget You altogether.
How will I ever find my way to You on this rutted road?

ABU-SAID ABIL-KHEIR, SUFI

The soul must find spiritual humility and avoid spiritual pride.
Such a soul, being in the state of misery,
never considers that it is making progress.
Thus the soul submits and becomes
obedient on the spiritual path.

JOHN OF THE CROSS, ROMAN CATHOLIC

Water and mind are both still.
Sun and moon reflect brightly.
Now and then a mist drifts across
my mirror like a cloud.
For a moment this confuses me,
but then I remember.

HSU YUN, ZEN BUDDHIST

Desires keep passing by and my vows seem empty.
Is life worth living if I am still trapped in illusions?
If we already know who we really are,
what is the point of playing life's childish games?

VLADIMIR SOLOVYOV, RUSSIAN ORTHODOX

In a serene state of mind there is
no recognition of good and bad fortune.
There is nothing to lose and nothing to gain.
This mirror is covered with a lifetime of dust.
Why not clean and polish it once and for all.

YOKA GENKAKU, ZEN BUDDHIST

There is no mirror, and no dust to wipe away.
Whoever understands this does not need to sit there all stiff.

G-KAN, ZEN BUDDHIST

Perceive what is in front of your face,
and that which is concealed from you will be revealed.

JESUS, *THE GOSPEL OF THOMAS*

One should give up trying to achieve anything by meditating.
Rather, see directly the reality at hand.

P'ANG YUN, CHAN BUDDHIST

I said to myself, "I have acquired great wisdom,
surpassing all who were over Jerusalem before me;
and my mind has had great experience of wisdom and knowledge."
And I applied my mind to know wisdom and to know
madness and folly.
I perceive that this also is but a striving after wind.
For in much wisdom is much vexation,
and he who increases knowledge increases sorrow.

ECCLESIASTES 1:6-18, THE BIBLE

With a torch and a bucket of water
I will set heaven ablaze and quell the fires of hell.
This way those seeking God can tear away the veil
and recognize the true goal.

RABI'A AL-ADAWIYYA, SUFI

Begin the quest now.
There will be no second chance.

RAHMAN BABA, SUFI

Effort is futile. Let God draw you to Him.
Forget yourself and lose yourself in Him.
This is the highest calling.

JACOPONE DA TODI, ROMAN CATHOLIC

My task is to open the eyes of man to see within—to eternity.
Lord give me your spirit of love and annihilate my selfhood.
Be the entirety of my life.

WILLIAM BLAKE

Early in my life I took the path of learning.
I read the scriptures, noticed the differences. I couldn't stop.
All this was in vain, for the eternal Buddha chastised me:
"What is the point of counting the treasure others have gained?"
Those many years were wasted—nothing but dust in the wind.

YUNG CHIA, CHAN BUDDHIST

It is easy to lose what God has given us.
Blessed are they who are firmly established here.

MECHTHILD OF MAGDEBURG, ROMAN CATHOLIC

I am neither free nor a slave.
I would not even know what to call myself
if my teacher hadn't given me a name.
I love no one else and no one loves me.
I just go where He drags me.

JELALUDDIN RUMI, SUFI

The whole world is at peace
when the mind is at peace.
Perceiving nothing as real or unreal,
not holding on to this or that reality,
not lingering in the void,
doing nothing holy, nothing wise.
I am just a run of the mill person who has finished his work.

P'ANG YUN, CHAN BUDDHIST

Realize that your karmic body is as vulnerable as a bubble.
All things are impermanent. Even in death you are helpless.
So hold no fantasies of eternity;
just make your life your work on the path,
and go to the place where illusion does not exist.

YESHE TSOGYEL, TIBETAN BUDDHIST

Keep seeking to understand
and you will become the mind of understanding.
If your life is lived for no other purpose
than to become the Essence one day,
then you become the Essence.
At the end of your journey you will discover
that you are what you have been searching for all along.

ABU-SAID ABU-KHEIR, SUFI

THE NARROW GATE

All religions are paths, but the paths are not God.

SRI RAMAKRISHNA, VEDANTA (HINDU)

Enter by the narrow gate;
for the gate is wide and the way is easy that leads to destruction,
and those who enter by it are many.
For the gate is narrow and the way is hard that leads to life,
and those who find it are few.

JESUS

The Great Way has no gate,
and there are thousands of paths to it.
If you set foot on the Way,
you will travel through the universe alone.

WU-MEN, CHAN BUDDHIST

The spiritual journey is unique to every individual.
You can't organize or direct it.
It isn't true that everyone should follow one path.
Listen to your own truth.

RAM DASS, VEDANTA (HINDU)

The wisdom of this world is foolishness with God.
The soul has to proceed by unknowing
rather than knowing.

JOHN OF THE CROSS, ROMAN CATHOLIC

Happiness begins when ambition ends.

THOMAS MERTON, ROMAN CATHOLIC

I relish this loss of a good reputation.
If some people scorn me and others honor me,
what does it matter?
Whatever others' opinions,
I will follow this one narrow path—
for on this path I have met the people of God.

MIRABAI, VEDANTA (HINDU)

Do not seek to follow in the footsteps
of the wise men of the past.
Rather, seek after what they sought.

MATSUO BASHO, ZEN BUDDHIST

If a man wishes to be sure of the road he treads on,
he must close his eyes and walk in the dark.

JOHN OF THE CROSS, ROMAN CATHOLIC

The spiritual path wrecks the body,
but restores it to health afterward.
The house must be destroyed so that
the treasure can be found beneath it.
And with that treasure the house will
be built better than before.

JELALUDDIN RUMI, SUFI

There is a man who lives in a ravine at the bottom of a mountain.
He wears clouds for a robe and sunset for tassels.
He has a gift he would share with others.
But the journey to this place was long and difficult,
and he has some regrets and doubts.
He is an old man now, and has never accomplished anything.
Others think he's crippled, but he is immovable and alone.

HAN-SHAN, TAOIST, CHAN BUDDHIST

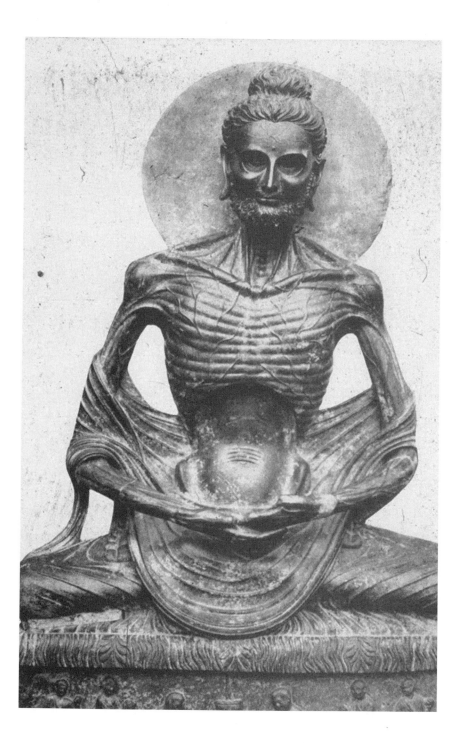

See all beings as equal. Recognize the Self in all.

THE SRIMAD BHAGAVATAM, HINDU SCRIPTURE

Spiritual perfection lies only at the end of a very long path.
Those who seek it become patient, knowing that
spiritual evolution is a process of gradual unfolding
over many millennia and countless incarnations.

SRI AUROBINDO, VEDANTA (HINDU)

Be dedicated and firm in all your actions,
but be easy in your heart.
Be strict with yourself, but be gentle with your fellow men.

TUT TUT

Be simple, plain, unselfish and have few desires.

LAO TZU, TAOIST

We seek, we dance, we have many ecstasies
and many great sorrows.
We will experience much pain and know great pleasure.
The stronger we become through all of this,
the more quickly we will achieve oneness in Nirvana.

J. KRISHNAMURTI

Without waiting or hesitating, and without
consideration of those around you, follow the Way
that is direct and straight and narrow.

THE EPISTULA APOSTOLORUM (AN EARLY CHRISTIAN MANUAL OF ORDER)

Learn to be gentle and you will overcome anger.
Be generous and you overcome selfishness.
Remain in truth and you will overcome meanness.
With truth, overcome pretense.

THE BUDDHA

To understand Zen,
be mindless wherever you are
and in everything you do.
Do this and you will naturally merge
with the Way.
The wise men of old called this
"The mind not touching things,
the steps not placed anywhere."

YIN-AN, ZEN BUDDHIST

If you wish to know the Way,
meditate and still the mind.
With knowledge comes perseverance,
and with perseverance comes knowledge.
The Way is neither full nor empty.
He who has a quiet mind understands this.
Tao is an empty vessel, an un-carved block.
Nothing is more mysterious.

LOY CHING-YUEN, TAOIST

Following the Great Way is easy
if you do not value one thing over another.
When extremes like love and hate are both absent,
one is able to see reality as it truly is.
But if you perceive differences between things,
then you will remain trapped in duality.
If you have likes and dislikes,
your mental peace will be disturbed to no purpose.

SENG TS'AN, CHAN BUDDHIST

On my mountain, I sit relaxed, cherishing simple things.
Incense burns, creating a mist that floats away before me.
As I roll down the blinds, I reflect on the moon in the pond.
I wonder how many of my old friends have known this Way?

ZENGETSU, ZEN BUDDHIST

If what you seek doesn't exist in any place,
why are you planning to travel to get there?
All you need do is polish the mirror within your own heart.
A mirror can only be polished with certain faith,
and the mind must be freed from hypocrisy, doubt and discord.

HAKIM ABU-AL-MAJD, SUFI

Within, my mind is clear and free of dust.
If it does not appear that way on the outside,
pay no attention.
I am climbing straight up the stairway to heaven.

T'AO CH'IEN, TAOIST

Ascending, the forest becomes darker.
Knowing becomes unknowing.
Knowing by unknowing reaches the Light
while reason crumbles in the darkness.
Scholars argue about such things,
but they never leave the ground.
The highest science is one that leads
to ecstasy in the unknowing.

JOHN OF THE CROSS, ROMAN CATHOLIC

The Way is not difficult for one who has no desires.

CHAO-CHOU TS'UNG-SHEN, CHAN BUDDHIST

Holding onto joy and sorrow,
love and hate,
passivity and anger,
lead one away from virtue and the Tao.
A heart that takes no notice
of opposites will remain unchanging,
and in perfect peace.
Do not relate to the duality
of the external world.
Avoid negative states of mind
if you wish to remain pure and unblemished.

CHUANG TZU, TAOIST

Your own thoughts can hurt you
far more that your worst enemy.
But once they are mastered they will help you
more than father or mother.

THE BUDDHA

It is important to give up expectations,
and to consider all experiences—
even the negative ones—
to be just another step on the path.
Then go forward.

RAM DASS, VEDANTA (HINDU)

The Buddha gave up running away from the
phenomenal world and simply returned to himself.
He became perfectly present to everything—
a single breath, the song of a bird, a falling leaf, the sun's rays.
Any of these things could serve him in meditation.
He came to understand that liberation
is attained with each step along the path.

THICH NHAT HANH, ZEN BUDDHIST

Give up the difficult path that appears in so many forms,
and walk alongside of Him who wants you to be free like I am.

JESUS, DIALOGUE OF THE SAVIOR, GNOSTIC-CHRISTIAN

Just as a mother who nurses her sick children
gives them each what they need according to their illness,
so God has given different paths to different people—
paths that are fitting to their natures.

SRI RAMAKRISHNA, VEDANTA (HINDU)

Let go of desires and simply act naturally;
just do what you do.
Who knows where the clouds of the sky,
or the water of a brook,
come from or where they are going.
There is no answer, so don't bother seeking it.

YUAN MEI, TAOIST

If you think the kingdom of God is in the sky,
then the birds of heaven will get there before you.
If you think it is in the sea, then the fish will find it before you do.

JESUS

Have no relationships with others.
Hold no desires in your heart.
When you no longer cling to things
and become strong and upright like a wall,
then you will begin walking the Path.

BODHIDHARMA, ZEN BUDDHIST

Do not ask God not to tempt you,
for how else will you overcome?
If you are surrounded by a wall of spirit,
what is there to fear?

JESUS, *THE APOCRYPHON OF JAMES*, GNOSTIC-CHRISTIAN

To find the Way to union, have no faith and no infidelity.
Step outside of yourself and see the Way.
Surrender to God entirely.
Then it no longer matters who you are with.
Not even a snake can harm you.
Just don't consort with yourself.

ABU-SAID ABIL-KHEIR, SUFI

You think that you have to find the Way
in order to understand your own nature.
Your nature is just what it is.
It was given to you, therefore it is perfect.
Trying to find proof of this causes you to
search in all the wrong places.
To pass over the trunk of a tree in order
to find the twigs will only make you stupid.

HAN SHAN, ZEN BUDDHIST

The goal is to be fully conscious—
to be aware of all your surroundings,
and to function within this reality.
But your consciousness should not
unite with the natural world.
Your inner awareness
should maintain independence.

RAMANA MAHARSHI, VEDANTA (HINDU)

Following the Buddha dharma,
I proceed on the non-Way
while conducting ordinary affairs in the world.
All that I experience I recognize as nameless
and without form.
Following this path I leave birth and death behind.

PANG YUN, CHAN BUDDHIST

My path is opening the heart by constant devotion to Him.
Doing so breaks down my resistance, so I cry all night.
Tears shed all night brought me to Him.

MIRABAI, VEDANTA (HINDU)

Life is the coming together of reality and dreams.
Such a union raises the human being to great heights.

DARSHAN SING, VEDANTA (HINDU)

If you give up everything you own,
you will experience a reality that is not of this world.
What you think is a place of power and position,
is really a prison.
Your lust for the things of this world makes it
impossible for you to leave good and evil behind.
Your hair turned white without your permission
and in the end your passions bring you to shame.

But if you give obeisance to God you will
receive kingdoms not of this world.
But your greatest joy will come simply from
turning over your will to Him.
Then you will experience true glory.

KABIR, SUFI

Anyone who turns his will and affairs over
entirely to God will have God with him in all
things that he does and experiences in life.

MEISTER ECKHART, ROMAN CATHOLIC

May you always have those things you hold dear,

and may you always do what you love.

But go forward swiftly, and lightly of step,

never swerving from the path to ultimate joy.

Do not believe or agree with anything that

discourages you from being resolute,

or causes you to stumble—

so that you may offer up your vows to God,

pursuing the path to perfection

to which the Lord has called you.

CLARE OF ASSISI, ROMAN CATHOLIC

By transforming yourself, you transform the world.
By finding the light within yourself, you bring light to all.

RAMANA MAHARSHI, VEDANTA (HINDU)

Truly loving God allows you to more easily
leave the world behind.
This was true of the apostles;
the greater their pain,
the easier it was to endure them.

MEISTER ECKHART, ROMAN CATHOLIC

Human thinking is like smoke given off to prove that fire exists.
A mystic sits in the middle of this fire and watches the myriad
of shapes that smoke takes on as it rises.
Enjoy the images, but don't leave the fire
to chase after the smoke.

JELALUDDIN RUMI, SUFI

There is no end to pleasures,
and as long as you float upon them
you are carried along from one lifetime to the next.
You run like a rabbit from a hunter,
pursued by your passions—from life to life.

THE BUDDHA

Life is a bridge. Cross over it,
don't install yourself upon it.

JESUS

As long as a person continues to strengthen the ego
by insisting on "This is who I am—this is mine,"
spiritual work will come to nothing.
When one turns their back on these two,
then they will die, and the work that God
has given us to do will be complete.
For true work is knowledge.
But when knowledge comes,
the work ceases to exist.

KABIR, SUFI

Whatever your actions, food or worship;
whatever the gift you have to give to another;
whatever your vow to the work of the Spirit . . .
give all these up as offerings to Me.

KRISHNA, THE BHAGAVAD GITA, VEDANTA

God flows inside creatures,
yet He remains untouched by all of them.
He has no need of them whatsoever.

PAUL TILLICH, PROTESTANT

To others, denying oneself and picking up your cross
means that we will fast and suffer.
I say that this means that we will be free from
suffering because nothing else follows this action except joy.

MEISTER ECKHART, ROMAN CATHOLIC

Like the Universe, the Way has no imperfections.
It requires nothing and contains only what it needs.
If one chooses to accept one thing and reject the other,
it is impossible to see the true nature of things.
Do not dwell in the complications of the world,
but don't remain in a state of emptiness either.
Accept that all things are one,
and incorrect views will vanish on their own.
If you try to stop actions in order to achieve
stillness, the effort to be still is itself action.
As long as you remain in one extreme
or the other you will never know Oneness.

SENG TS'AN, CHAN BUDDHIST

Love the Lord and you will achieve freedom.

He is the One who appears as many,

containing the entire cosmos,

and is without beginning or end.

Those with a pure heart can realize Him.

THE UPANISHADS, VEDANTA (HINDU)

As I walked on the road, you were my escort and guide.

If others asked me questions, it was You who answered.

When the sun set and the moon rose,

it was You who shined through the night.

You are the smile on my face, the verses I write,

and the songs I sing.

When I laughed, You were the smile on my face.

When I wrote, You were the verses.

When I sang, You were the song.

I rarely needed anyone else to love me,

but when I did, You came to me in them.

SARMAD, SUFI

All I do is go around trying to persuade others
not to give any thought to themselves or their possessions.
I encourage them, instead, to care about improving themselves—
especially the condition of their souls.

PLATO

With all this Light, there is nowhere to take my camel.
Wherever I go, I find the Lord.

SHAH ABDUL LATIF BHITAI, SUFI

The soul will continue to live in darkness
until the burning passions of the flesh are extinguished.
Desire is like a film covering an eye with dust.
Until the obstruction is removed,
it is impossible for the eye to see clearly.
The appetites of the flesh keep the soul
from being flooded with divine Light.
Even the smallest craving stains it.

JOHN OF THE CROSS, ROMAN CATHOLIC

I live on this deserted cliff apart from everything—
my loved ones, even myself.
This way I am able to concentrate only on Him.
Nothing else matters but to come into His presence.
Then there is ecstasy and bliss that far exceeds
earthly pleasures and joy.

VITTORIA DE COLONNA, PROTESTANT

Modern people are so obsessed with doing
that they have no time or imagination left for being.
Men are valued for what they do, not for what they have,
rather than for who they are.

THOMAS MERTON, ROMAN CATHOLIC

May my body, mind and abilities be used by You
in any way you choose to manifest Your will through me.
All work is Your work, and no task is too difficult or menial
when it is an offering in Your service.

PARAMAHANSA YOGANANDA, VEDANTA (HINDU)

I reached the unknown and remained there—
unknowing; going beyond human knowledge.
I could not find the door, but I found my way
through unknowing.
I entered the realm in which only holiness and peace exist.
I found the narrow path through solitude—deep within.
So far inside and far away, that I no longer experience
myself beyond the realm of the senses and feelings
I was so far inside, so dazed and far away,
my senses were released from feelings of my own.
My mind had found a surer way:
a knowledge of unknowing, rising beyond all science.

JOHN OF THE CROSS, ROMAN CATHOLIC

Those who truly seek the truth
directly from the heart of wisdom,
fly away from the passions which devour
the spirit in all living creatures.

THE BOOK OF THOMAS THE CONTENDER, GNOSTIC-CHRISTIAN

The wise man chooses to be least among others
and therefore becomes first.
He denies himself and therefore finds safety,
for one who is unselfish finds fulfillment.

LAO TZU, TAOIST

Everyone who glorifies himself will be humbled,
but one who humbles himself will be glorified.

JESUS

In love you found chastity. Reaching out, you found purity.
Accepting this, you became stronger, more generous,
more beautiful, more tender, more courteous.
And then He embraced you and adorned you with
sparkling gems that became blossoms which He placed
on your head as a golden crown, signifying your holiness.

CLARE OF ASSISI, ROMAN CATHOLIC

The masters of old did not desire life, nor seek death.
They entered the world without happiness
and left it without sadness.
Things come, things go.
They took life as it came, with joy.
They took death as it came, without fear.
They just went away—over there.

CHUANG TZU, TAOIST

Do what must be done,
but do it without attachment to the results.
Instead give all actions to God,
and evil will be banished naturally.

THE BHAGAVAD GITA, VEDANTA (HINDU)

The forest, the seas and the stars
lay within an earthen vessel—
and within that the Creator dwells.
That is where you will find the Lord, my friend—
within yourself.

KABIR, SUFI

I have set this old house ablaze and burned it down.
I carry a torch, and I'll burn your house down
if you want to follow me.

KABIR, SUFI

Tao is our guide as we pass through
this impermanent realm.
When pain and darkness come our way,
remember that all things are cyclical—
things come, things go.
In winter, know that spring will come again,
so be at peace within yourself.

LOY CHING-YUEN, TAOIST

Renounce the affairs of life, and practice.

This way you will help all those you meet along the way.

Seek solitude apart from others.

Go into the wild places;

for there you will find the hidden treasures

of happiness and joy.

SHABKAR, TIBETAN BUDDHIST

THE PATH WITHIN

Deluded, the musk deer searches everywhere
for the origin of the fragrance,
without realizing it lies within himself.
This is the way it is for those who go
on pilgrimages and follow religious observances.
If you wish to find your home,
look within.
If you wish to find the Lord,
seek Him within yourselves.
This is true wisdom.

DARIYA, VEDANTA (HINDU)

If you wish to find what you are looking for,
remove that which hides your heart.

KABIR, SUFI

If you wish to obtain true knowledge,
then grasp the oneness that dwells within yourself.
The cleansed mirror waits within—waiting for you.

HADEWIJCH, ROMAN CATHOLIC

If you want the treasure,
don't look for it outside of yourself.
You already carry it within,
so why not use it without restraint?

MA-TSU TAO I, CHAN BUDDHIST

The flower contains the fragrance within itself.
Just so, the Lord resides in you.
You need not look elsewhere.

GURU NANAK, VEDANTA (HINDU)

Your teacher will introduce your true teacher to you—
the one that lies within your own consciousness.

SWAMI RAMA, VEDANTA (HINDU)

The Kingdom is within you, and whoever knows
oneself will find it. All those who find the kingdom
will know that they are heirs of the Father.
Know that you are in God, and God is in you.

JESUS, PAPYRUS OXYRHYNCHUS I

All the scriptures tell us the same thing: "Know thyself."
If you have known yourself, you have known everything else.
The Bible says, "Seek that kingdom within you."
It is not outside. Once you have found That,
then all other things will be added to you.

SWAMI SATCHIDANANDA, VEDANTA (HINDU)

To find a Buddha, all you have to do is see your own nature.

BODHIDHARMA, ZEN BUDDHIST

Our soul was created to be the dwelling place of God,
and that indwelling *is* God.

JULIANA OF NORWICH, ROMAN CATHOLIC

The seeker becomes the knower because
the thing to be known is already there.
There is nothing else to know.
And there are not two things,
because the seeker is both the
knower and the known.

RAMANA MAHARSHI, VEDANTA (HINDU)

He is a scoundrel, that yogi.

For him, there is no earth or sky—no form of any kind.

He sets up shop in a marketplace that does not exist.

He weighs things and manages accounts.

But he has no deed, no yogic powers, no religion,

not even a bowl to go begging with.

I am you and you are me, and I'm inside of you.

SRI RAMAKRISHNA, VEDANTA (HINDU)

God plants a seed deep inside of you,

and that seed is Himself.

If you are a bright and hard working fellow,

the seed will grow,

and become a full blooming plant,

which is God.

With the right conditions and constant nurturing,

the seed of every plant grows up to be that plant.

God seeds grow up to be

the One who planted the seed.

MEISTER ECKHART, ROMAN CATHOLIC

Do not judge, simply be a witness.

Focus on yourself, not others.

Don't listen to the crowd,

listen to what your own heart tells you.

MA-TSU, ZEN BUDDHIST

The One who created all things,

holds all things within Himself.

He also has a special dwelling place,

and that dwelling place is within your own heart.

EDITH STEIN, ROMAN CATHOLIC

If God could be found by ritual cleansing,

then frogs and fish can find Him.

If God could be found deep in the forest or in the fields,

then cows would have found him by now.

But God is found by those who have a pure heart.

BULLEH SHAH, SUFI

The center of divine knowledge
exists within every human being.
When one finds that center, one naturally
becomes a poet without ever having
studied the art of poetry.

Swami Muktananda, Vedanta (Hindu)

People can sit still on a cushion for many years
without ever finding ultimate Truth.
If you are looking for the supreme Tao,
look inside yourself—
because it has always been there.

Lu Tung-Pin, Taoist

Fish don't get thirsty because water exists in them,
so why do people say they cannot find the answer
when it already resides within them?
Travel to one holy city after another if you wish,
but you will never discover that which is real.

Kabir, Sufi

The body is the house in which the spirit resides.

JELALUDDIN RUMI, SUFI

Those people who search for the Buddha
outside of their own mind,
will never find him.

BODHIDHARMA, ZEN BUDDHIST

The moment I have truly realized God
sitting in the temple of every human heart,
the moment I revere every human being as God—
that is the moment when I am set free from bondage.

SWAMI VIVEKANANDA, VEDANTA (HINDU)

You can travel to the four corners of the earth,
but you will not find anything anywhere.
Whatever is there, is already here.

SRI RAMAKRISHNA, VEDANTA (HINDU)

When you are already in Detroit,
you don't have to take a bus to get there.

RAM DASS, VEDANTA (HINDU)

I am rich because I have nothing.
Can I say that I am thirsty when
water surrounds me on all sides?
How do I grasp the One I see every day,
when he is within me—yet invisible
and beyond all worlds?

SYMEON THE NEW THEOLOGIAN, EASTERN ORTHODOX

The only true mosque is the one that
is built in the hearts of saints.
This is the place for worship,
because this is where God dwells.

JELALUDDIN RUMI, SUFI

There is no difference between God, Guru and the Self.

RAMANA MAHARSHI, VEDANTA (HINDU)

To one who realizes God,
there is no difference between
the Spirit and the senses.
God is seen, but He is also heard,
tasted, felt and smelled.

ANGELUS SILESIUS, ROMAN CATHOLIC

Our rational minds can never understand what has
happened, but our hearts . . . if we can keep them
open to God, will find their own intuitive way.

RAM DASS, VEDANTA (HINDU)

The only really valuable thing is intuition.

ALBERT EINSTEIN

Direct your eye inward,
and you'll find a thousand regions
of your mind yet undiscovered.

HENRY DAVID THOREAU

Working at my desk, my mind calm as a lake without wind,
I was suddenly struck with something akin to a crash of thunder.
Immediately my inner vision was released and I saw my ordinary self.

LAYMAN SEIKEN, ZEN BUDDHIST

There is nothing wrong with seeking happiness.
It is our birthright.
The problem is where we look for it:
outside of us instead of inside.

RAMANA MAHARSHI, VEDANTA (HINDU)

All can hear the still small voice within.
Be still and know that I Am within you as God,
the Beloved. Listen, and live by it.

EILEEN CADDY

Within this container of flesh lies forests and groves,
and within those, God dwells.
Within this container of flesh also lies the seven seas
and countless stars.
And within them dwells God.
Truly, my Beloved lies within.

KABIR, SUFI

RELINQUISHING THE EGO

There is knowledge that cannot be known
until one lets go of the ego.
I let go of my ego and
became one with Shiva and Shakti.

JANADEV, VEDANTA (HINDU)

The spiritual path is not about being somebody—
it is about being nobody.

RAM DASS, VEDANTA (HINDU)

One must perceive that the personal ego
does not exist if he is to reach the final goal.

MILAREPA, TIBETAN BUDDHIST

You cut him, Lord, yet he does not smell of blood.

You burn him but he does not stink of smoke.

The one that burns just laughs.

The one who dies just cries out with joy.

KHWAJA ABDULLAH ANSARI, SUFI

Do not be concerned for me.

Though they say I suffered,

I did not suffer in any way.

For I am He who was within me

from the beginning.

JESUS, *THE FIRST APOCALYPSE OF JAMES*, GNOSTIC-CHRISTIAN

The one you see beside the cross laughing—

he is the living Jesus.

The one whose hands and feet are nailed

to the tree is nothing more than his image in flesh.

THE COPTIC GNOSTIC APOCALYPSE OF PETER, GNOSTIC-CHRISTIAN

When will I be free?
When "I" am no more.

SRI RAMAKRISHNA, VEDANTA (HINDU)

There are two selves: the separate ego-self
and the Self that is the imperishable Atman.
When one rises above the "I"-self, Atman is
then realized to be the true Self.

THE KATHA UPANISHAD, VEDANTA (HINDU)

The ego-self and the Self exist in the same body.
The ego-self judges between good and evil,
while the other Self does not discriminate.
As long as we believe we are the ego-self, we will suffer.
But when we realize that we are the true Self,
the very Lord, then we are freed from suffering
and attain a state of bliss.

THE MUNDAKA UPANISHAD, VEDANTA (HINDU)

I became lost in the city of love,

and there my soul was cleansed.

Gradually I disappeared from myself—

first my head, then my hands and feet.

When the ego had entirely vanished,

I reached the highest goal.

BULLEH SHAH, SUFI

This ruler over me sensed its own death.

It becomes silent and weak and then flees.

Let it flee, let it die, this cold and arrogant ruler.

I am the priest, and I am the sacrifice.

I remain safe within the sanctuary as I watch

the end of this torturer.

Now I stand before You, besieged with bliss.

VLADIMIR SOLOVYOV, RUSSIAN ORTHODOX

Rising through the many realms,
the Soul said to its interrogator,
"The chains that bound me have been broken.
The walls of ignorance that surrounded me have crumbled.
My cravings have ended and my ignorance dispelled.
Now I am free.
From this moment forward I rest forever in silence.

THE GOSPEL OF MARY (MAGDALENE), GNOSTIC-CHRISTIAN

The ego says I "exist."
My heart says, "I am less than that."
My spirit says, "You are nothing at all."

THEODORE ROETHKE

The self tastes sweet and bitter,
and prefers the first over the second.
The supreme Self has no preference.
The self stumbles in the darkness,
while the supreme Self walks in the light.

THE KATHA UPANISHAD, VEDANTA (HINDU)

He who seeks learning, gains each day.

He who seeks Tao decreases each day.

He will continue to decrease until he

comes to non-action.

Without acting, everything is accomplished.

THE TAO TE CHING, TAOIST

Following Buddhism, one studies the mind until

he forgets the mind and becomes enlightened.

When body and mind drop away,

enlightenment disappears.

From then on, there is no trace of anyone.

DOGEN, ZEN BUDDHIST

We are the veil that hides God from ourselves.

HAZRAT INAYAT KHAN, SUFI

Put the veil in front of my face, and I'll disappear.
Yet I am as close to you as always.
So it is with God and the ego.

SRI RAMAKRISHNA, VEDANTA (HINDU)

Love came and drained me of myself.
I became a container for the Beloved.
Nothing is left but a name.
Everything else is the Beloved.

ABU-SAID ABIL-KHEIR, SUFI

The teacher went from house to house
carrying a lamp and knocking on doors.
When they opened, he asked,
"Is there no one here?
He's who I'm looking for."

JELALUDDIN RUMI, SUFI

Lose the ego and you will find everything.
Then you will begin to become what you truly are.

ANDREW COHEN

Consider yourself to be nothing.
Completely forget yourself and
your troubles when you pray.
Pray only for Divine Presence.
Then you will enter a realm beyond time
where all separateness ceases to exist.

MAGGID OF MERZERITCH, JEWISH

Bathing in the Light of Truth within myself
I gave up planning and plotting.
If you, too, have a hint of the transcendent,
then flee from yourself and see that you are
the splendor of God.

SARMAD, SUFI

One can learn to let go of the ego's desire
to save the world and surrender everything to God.
Ego projects a world that is illusory,
and no such world exists.

DAVID HAWKINS

The ego is nothing more than
the focus of conscious attention.

ALAN WATTS, ZEN BUDDHIST

As long as you are aware that "you" exists,
that it knows, that it possesses and values,
you are still in bondage.

ANGELUS SILESIUS, ROMAN CATHOLIC

The true Self within never changes,
while the individual intellect is never conscious.
Seeing the world, the observer says,
"It is I who sees, I who knows," never suspecting
that this is a delusion of the mind.
But if one recognizes his true self as not
being the individual ego, but the supreme Self,
he ceases to experience fear.

SHANKARA, VEDANTA (HINDU)

Death is the stripping away of all that is not you.
The secret of life is to "die before you die"—
and then there is no death.

ECKHART TOLLE

I have held onto things so tightly.
Now I just want them to fall apart.

SAKYON MISHRAM RIMPOCHE, TIBETAN BUDDHIST

If you don't first get rid of yourself you will meet
one obstacle after another wherever you go.
Those who look for peace outside of themselves—
in anything at all, no matter how great—will never find it.
The more one seeks this way, the more deluded he becomes.
But the person who completely forsakes himself
has abandoned even those things he keeps.
The more you lose yourself, the more room you have for God.

MEISTER ECKHART, ROMAN CATHOLIC

As long as you cling to yourself
you will wander around for countless ages—
gaining nothing.
But the day the scales of ego fall from your eyes,
you will see that your wandering has no purpose.
Once freed from delusion of individuality,
the door will open to you within minutes.

HAKIM ABU-AL-MAJD, SUFI

In order to recognize the non-existence of individual ego,
the mind must become still.
In this state, the thinking mind ceases to be active,
and true mind becomes serene.
In this state of tranquility,
one does not recognize the passage of time,
so others have to keep track of it for him.

MILAREPA, TIBETAN BUDDHIST

If you find it impossible to get rid of "I,"
then make your ego a "servant-I."
The "I" that is the servant of God does
not get into too much mischief.

SRI RAMAKRISHNA, VEDANTA (HINDU)

I came to see the Dharma-body of the Buddha
in everything the Not-I looked at.

ALDOUS HUXLEY

When one sees all things in their totality,
he recognizes that all things are perfect as they are,
and nothing from the outside is needed to change anything.
The limited ego thinks the world is in need of fixing,
but this is an illusion and a vanity.

DAVID HAWKINS

Though I seem to suffer in darkness,
love has changed my soul so that
I burn myself away—
and am wholly consumed.

JOHN OF THE CROSS, ROMAN CATHOLIC

In our tradition, we break coconuts before God
as a symbol of our breaking of the ego.
Just as sweet water flows out of a broken coconut,
joy flows out of us when we relinquish the ego.

SWAMI SUKHABODHANANDA, VEDANTA (HINDU)

As nothing, I see all.
The streams of Universal Being flow through me.
I am just a grain of God.

RALPH WALDO EMERSON

Let go of all that is negative in you.
Surrender the ego,
and then you will experience bliss.

SATHYA SAI BABA, VEDANTA (HINDU)

Returning to a place he had experienced joy many years before,
the traveler demanded nothing and expected nothing—
wanting only to see with clarity that place where this is not I.

CZESLAW MILOSZ

PRAYER

—※—

Vivekananda taught that if one has a selfless, noble, thought—
even deep in a cave, such thought creates vibrations that
affect the entire world—
and accomplishes what can be accomplished.

RAMANA MAHARSHI, VEDANTA (HINDU)

—※—

It is my nature to love Him, so I love.
I don't pray for anything, or ask for anything.
I just let Him do with me as He wills.

SWAMI VIVEKANANDA, VEDANTA (HINDU)

What is prayer other than a projection of yourself into the ether?
If it comforts you to tell of your darkness to the cosmos,
or if it is your delight to pour forth your joy,
then let your soul call you again and again to prayer—
so that you might weep and weep, until your sorrow turns to joy.

KAHLIL GIBRAN

I kneel in the universal temple of my heart.
I pray at the altar where walls and names do not exist.

RABI'A AL-ADAWIYYA, SUFI

The prayer of the monk is not perfect
until he no longer recognizes himself
or the fact that he is praying.

ST. ANTHONY, ROMAN CATHOLIC

Prayer is the key to the morning
And the bolt of the evening.

MAHATMA GANDHI

In sacred hymns and order,
the great chime and symphony of nature,
Prayer is the world in tune, a spirit-voice,
whose echo is heaven's bliss.

HENRY VAUGHN

The most powerful form of prayer is the one
that does not seek its own interest,
but is simply immersed in God's will.

MEISTER ECKHART, ROMAN CATHOLIC

If you pray with sincerity,
your prayers are already answered—
otherwise you have gained nothing.
Prayers that are mere repetition,
or the words of another, are worthless.

HAKIM ABU-AL-MAJD, SUFI

When you pray, do not pray as the hypocrites do,

for they love to stand in public and on the street corners

so that they can be seen by others. This is their reward.

Rather, when you pray, go into your secret chamber

and shut your door. And your Father, who is in secret

and hears in secret, will reward you openly.

And in praying, do not heap up empty phrases as the Gentiles do, for

they think they will be heard for their

many words. Do not be like them because your Father

knows what you need before you ask Him.

JESUS

God, grant me the serenity to accept the things I cannot change,

the courage to change the things I can,

and the wisdom to distinguish one from the other.

REINHOLD NIEBUHR, PROTESTANT

In prayer, while a man's mouth and lips are moving,
his heart and will must soar to the height of heights,
so as to acknowledge the unity of the whole, in virtue
of the mystery of mysteries in which all ideas, all wills,
and all thoughts, find their goal.

THE ZOHAR, JEWISH

May He who is known in all religions
lead us from the unreal to the Real,
from darkness into light,
from death to immortality.
And may He manifest himself in us as love.

SWAMI AKHILANANDA, VEDANTA (HINDU)

I pray to that Mystery that makes no distinctions.

DERVA DASIMAYYA, VEDANTA (HINDU)

I have learned to pray thus:
You, my very soul, trust in me,
for I shall never betray you.

RAINER MARIA RILKE

Let your mind be filled with Me,
and become devoted to Me.
Unite your heart with Mine.
See Me as the ultimate Goal.
Filled with Me, you will come to Me.

KRISHNA, THE BHAGAVAD GITA, VEDANTA (HINDU)

I sing my love for You.

I repeat Your name without ceasing.

I bring Your glory into my heart.

I am the lotus of love floating on the waters of God.

When I repeat your name and I find life.

When I forget, I die.

Guru Nanak, Vedanta (Hindu)

Lord, let us empty ourselves of doctrines.

Lao Tzu, Taoist

THE ESSENTIAL MYSTICS, POETS, SAINTS, AND SAGES

May I be free from fear.
May I be free from suffering.
May I be happy.
May I be filled with loving kindness.
May you be free from fear.
May you be free from suffering.
May you be happy.
May you be filled with loving kindness.
May all people everywhere be happy
and filled with loving kindness.

BUDDHIST PRAYER

I believe in the sun, even when it is not shining.
I believe in love, even when I don't feel it.
I believe in God even when He/She is silent.

JEWISH PRAYER

You, whose light penetrates the darkness
and dispels all illusions,
pour forth upon us Your perfect love,
Your supreme joy and Your everlasting peace.

SUFI PRAYER

Lord, make me an instrument of thy peace.

Where there is hatred, let me sow love.

Where there is injury, pardon;

Where there is doubt, faith;

Where there is despair, hope;

Where there is darkness, light.

O divine master, may I not so much seek

to be consoled as to console,

to be loved as to love,

to be understood as to understand.

For it is in giving that we receive.

It is in pardoning that we are pardoned,

and it is in dying,

that we are born to eternal life.

FRANCIS OF ASSISI, ROMAN CATHOLIC

May all living beings,

both visible and invisible,

those far from us and near,

those living in the world and those waiting to be born—

attain inner peace.

THE BUDDHA

When praying, it is more worthwhile to lift up a heart without words,
than it is to speak words without heart.

MAHATMA GANDHI

May we, in mutual love, become one spirit with Him.

BEATRICE OF NAZARETH, ROMAN CATHOLIC

From the point of light within the Mind of God,
let light stream forth into the minds of men.
Let light descend on earth.

ALICE BAILEY AND DJWHAL KHUL, THEOSOPHY

We give thanks to You!
Every soul and heart is lifted up to You,
From you, our Father, comes all fatherly kindness.
From You, our Mother, residing in the womb of all beings
and pregnant with the All, comes all love.
Grant us mind so that we may perceive You,
speech so that we may speak of You,
knowledge so that we may know You.
Of Thee we ask only one thing:
that we may be steadfast in our love,
and stumble not upon the path to You.

FROM THE *HERMETIC PRAYER OF THANKSGIVING*

In reverence, we offer sweet blooming flowers
which today are fresh and sweet and tomorrow,
like our bodies, will pass away.
We offer candles so that Your light may shine
in the hearts of all beings.
We offer incense so that Your sweet fragrance
may spread throughout the world.

FROM THE PALI CANON, THERAVADA BUDDHIST

You who are Light, enlighten us.
You who are Wisdom, help us to be wise.
You who are all Strength, make us strong.
We ask only that we may know your truth
and follow it with a simple heart.

CATHERINE OF SIENA, ROMAN CATHOLIC

Give me profound thoughts and elevated dreams.
Let me have few words and guide me on the narrow Path,
so that at the end of my journey I might find peace.

HAZRAT INAYAT KHAN, SUFI

Let me protect the helpless, guide the traveler,
enlighten those in darkness, and provide shelter
for those who are homeless.
Let me be a servant of all, and a bridge for those
who want to cross over to the other shore.

MAHAYANA BUDDHIST PRAYER

CONTEMPLATION AND MEDITATION

—⌇⌇—

Be still and know that I Am.

PSALM 46, THE BIBLE

—⌇⌇—

With meditation comes wisdom.
Lack of meditation maintains ignorance.
Use those things that are helpful to your progress
and avoid those that stand in your way.
You the traveler: choose the path to wisdom.

THE BUDDHA

—⌇⌇—

Meditation is not the means to an end.
It is both the means and the end.

J. KRISHNAMURTI

Meditation dissolves thought
and allows for pure consciousness that
goes beyond objectifying the outer world.
It is a merging of the finite with the infinite.

SWAMI SIVANANDA, VEDANTA (HINDU)

Meditation should not be confused
with that which you do in the morning.
That's practice,
while mediation is the result of that practice.

YOGI BHAJAN, VEDANTA (HINDU)

If you wish to meet the lord, then practice solitude.
Center the mind on a single point and become
free of all thought.
Little by little you will replace grief with happiness
and confusion with clarity.

SARMAD, SUFI

The purpose of meditation is to calm the mind.
But if you are already calm, why meditate?
Meditation is a kind of preventive medicine.
It can also serve you when your mind becomes agitated.
But don't be disappointed if you are unable to meditate
successfully in the beginning.
You must learn to walk before you can run.
Leaning to meditate is a gradual process.

SWAMI SATCHIDANANDA, VEDANTA (HINDU)

Mindfulness is the key to meditation,
as well as continuous effort.
Do not expect results right away.
Just keep practicing.

TENZIN GYATSO, HIS HOLINESS THE FOURTEENTH DALAI LAMA,
TIBETAN BUDDHIST

It is important to give one's attention to just one thing at a time.
With enough practice you will learn how to direct your attention
anywhere you choose.

EKNATH EASWARAN, VEDANTA (HINDU)

THE ESSENTIAL MYSTICS, POETS, SAINTS, AND SAGES

Empty your heart and mind, and sit quietly on a mat.
In meditation we become one with All.

LOY CHING-YUEN, TAOIST

That which a man gains from meditation
he should spend in love.

MEISTER ECKHART, ROMAN CATHOLIC

Let go of all matters and concerns.
Zazen is non-thinking.
It is not looking within.
Drop your desire to become a Buddha.
Let everything drop away.

DOGEN, ZEN BUDDHIST

If you wish to triumph over fear,

meditation is the way.

It is the only way.

By identifying with the One,

we identify with the vastness of all that is.

All things and people are a part of us,

and we are part of everything and everyone else.

So there is nothing outside of us to fear.

So how can we fear ourselves?

SRI CHINMOY, VEDANTA (HINDU)

With unwavering attention we see all the wonders that exist—

everything around us, above us, below us.

This pure sight exists in you.

Then all that exists, exists in you.

VLADIMIR SOLOVYOV, RUSSIAN ORTHODOX

People can spend their entire lives sitting on a cushion with their eyes closed. Their posture may be correct. Their breathing may be correct. Yet if they die without ever having practiced meditation in the physical world, then they have made no progress. Meditation must be part of everything you do. You must act from inner awareness and peace. Most importantly, you must be the witness of what is being done. Then you will be a true meditator.

SWAMI SAI PREMANANDA, VEDANTA (HINDU)

Meditation means giving up all your
pre-conceived notions and prejudices.
Nothing should stand in the way of direct awareness.
Meditation is seeing without thought.
Don't let the Buddha, Krishna or Christ
stand in the way of you seeing clearly.

J. KRISHNAMURTI

One can unite with God through faith.
But contemplation is a means for the intellect
to achieve a higher knowledge of God.
This mystical path will lead to His hidden wisdom.

JOHN OF THE CROSS, ROMAN CATHOLIC

Meditation is not about getting out of ourselves
or achieving something better.
It is about getting in touch with what you already are.

PEMA CHÖDRÖN, TIBETAN BUDDHIST

If you want to know where the best place to meditate is,
I'd recommend meditating in grassy fields and meadows.
Grass will awaken the heart.

NACHMAN OF BRATZLAV, JEWISH

Meditation is very difficult in the beginning,
but it promises bliss and joy in the end.

SWAMI SIVANANDA, VEDANTA (HINDU)

Meditation is a level of consciousness
in which "I" and "mine" have disappeared.
It is their absence that allows the mind to achieve order.

J. KRISHNAMURTI

The prophets meditate within their own hearts,
and watch their thoughts change in substance.
This process is subjective, but God's light illumines their thoughts.
This light emanates from outside the subjective mind.
But it does not result in words that can be understood.
It is simply light.
From this point on, one may transcend to higher and higher realms of
light until the mind of one who meditates reaches its divine destination.

ABRAHAM BEN SAMUEL ABULAFIA, JEWISH

Meditation essentially mean awareness.
Whenever you are completely aware, this is meditation.
It can be done while walking and listening to birds with your full
attention.
Just giving direct attention to the chatter of your mind is meditation.

OSHO, VEDANTA (HINDU)

In secret I spoke with the wise one, and I asked,
"Tell me the world's secrets."
The wise one replied, "Hush, and listen to the silence.
Silence will reveal all things to you."

JELALUDDIN RUMI, SUFI

I meditate in order to defeat the fiery monster of desire.

WANG WE, TAOIST

Music without words is like meditation.
It takes you directly to the source of sound
and leaves the mind behind.

KABIR, SUFI

If you want water to run faster,
remove all obstructions.
There is little more you need to do.

YOGASWAMI, VEDANTA (HINDU)

One's desire for God, if uncontrolled,
can obstruct the soul from reaching its goal.
The desire for God must come from a place of stillness.
It must become passive,
yet embody the intensity of one's heart and mind.

ALDOUS HUXLEY

The soul naturally longs to meditate
because it wishes to commune with the Spirit.
If you experience a mental resistance in meditation,
just remember that what resists is the ego, not the soul.

PARAMAHANSA YOGANANDA, VEDANTA (HINDU)

We cannot see the stars in the daytime,
but we know they exist.
When clouds obscure the sun,
we know the sun still exists.
Though you cannot see God with your eyes,
He does exist.
In order to see God one must develop
an inner eye through the practice of meditation.
With your eyes closed, and your senses
cut off from sensual objects,
seek God with your full attention, devotion and love.
You will surely find Him waiting for you with open arms.
Your body is His temple. Your heart is the holy of holies.

SWAMI SIVANANDA, VEDANTA (HINDU)

Go within yourself, and what you achieve there
will overshadow your imperfections.

SRI CHINMOY, VEDANTA (HINDU)

This staff, as you see, is just a staff.
When you move, it is just movement.
When you sit, it is just sitting.
But take care not to wobble.

YUN-MEN, CHAN BUDDHIST

He who is always content and contemplative,
with his passions subdued,
with his heart and mind devoted to me,
is made holy by Me, and cherished by Me.

KRISHNA, THE BHAGAVAD GITA, VEDANTA (HINDU)

Create yourself anew in the likeness of the Godhead.
In deepest contemplation experience the invisible
sweetness of His divine revelation
to all those who seek Him.

CLARE OF ASSISI, ROMAN CATHOLIC

Let your heart become ever more humble
so that you may give of yourself equally to all.
Then you will be capable of meditating.

ISAAC OF ACCO, JEWISH

I tried to find you in the gentle winds of dawn,
in the fragrance of a flower in the garden of Eden.
But I could find you only deep within myself
through contemplation.

SARMAD, SUFI

I placed in the ground my vine of love.
I watered it in silence with my tears.
Now it has grown and overspread my dwelling.
You offered me a cup of poison
which I drank with joy.
Mira is absorbed in contemplation of Krishna.
She is with God and all is well.

MIRABAI, VEDANTA (HINDU)

Those who look for the Beloved
will find Him in stillness,
rather than in the frenzied activity of daily life.

SARMAD, SUFI

If there is joy in meditation upon the sun and moon,
the planets and fixed stars are the magic creation
of the sun and moon;
make yourself like the sun and the moon themselves.

MILAREPA, TIBETAN BUDDHIST

Since nothing is understood particularly in that substantial quietude,
one might feel they are wasting their time.
The less they understand, the further they penetrate
into the night of the spirit. They must pass through
this night to a union with God beyond all knowing.
Another sign is the loving, general knowledge or awareness of God.
A person might remain in deep oblivion and
afterwards will think no time has passed at all.
This oblivion is caused by the purity and simplicity of the knowledge.
The effects are an elevation of mind to heavenly knowledge,
a withdrawal and abstraction from all objects,
forms and figures as well as from the remembrance of them.
The soul knows only God without knowing how it knows Him.

JOHN OF THE CROSS, ROMAN CATHOLIC

You are the forest, the great trees,
the birds and beasts playing within.
O Lord, white as jasmine,
You who fill and are filled.
Why don't you show me your Face?

AKKA MAHADEVI, VEDANTA (HINDU)

Happy is the portion of whoever can penetrate into
the mysteries of his master
and become absorbed into him as it were.
Especially does a man achieve this when he
offers up his prayer to his master in intense devotion,
his will then becoming, as the flame, inseparable from the goal,
and his mind concentrates on the unity of the higher firmaments,
and finally on the absorption of them all into the most high firmament.
Whilst a man's mouth and lips are moving,
his hearing and will must soar to the height
of heights, so as to acknowledge the unity of the whole,
in virtue of the mystery of mysteries in which all ideas,
and all thoughts find their goal.

MOSES BEN SHEM TOV, JEWISH

Meditation is dangerous for it destroys everything.
Nothing whatsoever is left,
not even a whisper of desire,
and in this vast, unfathomable emptiness
there is creation and love.

J. KRISHNAMURTI

The secret of the receptive must be sought in stillness:
within stillness there remains the potential for action.
If you force empty sitting, holding dead images in mind,
the tiger runs, the dragon flees—how can the elixir be given?

SUN BU-ER, CHAN BUDDHIST, TAOIST

If you try to stop the mind,
it will only become more active.
It is not necessary to stop it.
You must ask it where it is going.

YOGASWAMI, VEDANTA (HINDU)

When you have entirely surrendered,
everything you do will be meditation.

YOGASWAMI, VEDANTA (HINDU)

LOVE AND COMPASSION

―――※※※―――

Love one another as I have loved you.

JESUS

―――※※※―――

Love is the reality, and it is not a mere emotion.
It is the great Truth that lies behind all of creation.

RABINDRANATH TAGORE, VEDANTA (HINDU)

―――※※※―――

If you wish to become a pilgrim
Treading the path of love,
you must first find great humility and
become nothing more than dust and ashes.

JELALUDDIN RUMI, SUFI

I'm not interested in being a "lover,"
I'm only interested in *being* love.

RAM DASS, VEDANTA (HINDU)

Because of those who were sick, I became sick.
Because of those who were hungry, I hungered.
Because of those who were thirsty, I was athirst.

FRAGMENT OF A LOST GOSPEL

Hate cannot be conquered by hate.
Hate can only be conquered by love.
This is eternal law.
Many do not know how we come
to be here in this existence,
but those who do, cease quarreling immediately.

THE BUDDHA

If we truly feel the suffering of others,

as well as the happiness of others,

then we are loving God.

MEHER BABA, SUFI

If you wish to know who I belong to, I belong to love.

She embraces me so completely

that I can do nothing except through her.

MARGUERITE PORETE, ROMAN CATHOLIC

What can hide love, when a tear proclaims it loudly?

Those without love grasp at everything,

while the loving serves others.

Where is love?

It is said that the soul is contained within flesh and bone,

and that love comes from this innermost region.

And from this love within comes enlightenment.

A loveless life is like a tree that has wasted away

under a baking sun.

To find love, hold onto the One who holds onto nothing,

and in this holding, cease to cling to this life.

TIRUVALLUVAR, VEDANTA (HINDU)

Love has overpowered me.

This comes as no surprise,

for she is strong and I am weak.

Love rules my life and does with me as she wills.

What I was, I no longer am—for I have ceased to be.

Once I was rich, now I am poor,

for I have lost everything to love.

HADEWIJCH, ROMAN CATHOLIC

One who opens his heart to love,

sacrifices his own soul,

for from that moment forward,

his life is beyond reason's control.

FARID UD-DIN ATTAR, SUFI

Love is the true light of this world.

It instructs us, informs us,

and sets our heart on fire.

It unites us with God incarnate.

JACOPONE DA TODI, ROMAN CATHOLIC

Come near to His ear and share

the deepest longings of your heart.

Let the Beloved take up residence there.

KABIR, SUFI

You have heard that it was said,
"You shall love your
neighbor and hate your enemy."
But I say to you,
Love your enemies and pray for those who persecute you, so
that you may be sons of your Father who is in heaven;
for he makes the sun rise on the evil and on the good alike,
and sends rain on the just and the unjust.
For if you love only those who love you,
what reward have you?
Do not even the tax collectors do the same?
And if you salute only your brethren,
what more are you doing than others?
Do not even the Gentiles do the same? You, therefore,
must be perfect, as your heavenly Father is perfect.

JESUS, THE GOSPEL OF MATTHEW

I am nothing more than a speck of dust,
an atom of Jesus who dwells
in the prison of love.

THÉRÈSE OF LISIEUX, ROMAN CATHOLIC

One who loves all the world
as if it were his own flesh and blood,
can be relied upon to rule an empire.

LAO TZU, TAOIST

Love burns away the impurities of the soul
until it is wholly transformed.

JOHN OF THE CROSS, ROMAN CATHOLIC

Love is infectious.
Those who lack it can catch it from others.
Religions, worship, penance, even meditation
are not necessarily signs that a person has love.
Love sets one on fire so that
nothing comes out of his mouth but smoke.

MEHER BABA, SUFI

We go through one incarnation after another
like ghosts drifting from room to room.
We seek love in others,
yet rarely find it as advertised.
We pass from dream to dream
until we finally awaken to love.

STEVEN LEVINE

The wise man does no harm to others,
but takes no credit for his love and mercy.
He has no interest in worldly things,
but he does not scorn those who do.

CHUANG TZU, TAOIST

Love is not about giving and receiving.
Loving is the ability to see the Beloved
in everyone around us.

RAM DASS, VEDANTA (HINDU)

We should be grateful for the poor
because they allow us to help them.
We should be grateful that we are allowed
to spread love and mercy in the world,
because through loving we become perfect.

SWAMI VIVEKANANDA, VEDANTA (HINDU)

Love your neighbor as yourself.

LEVITICUS, THE BIBLE, JEWISH

Love unites what is divided,
Makes what is bitter sweet,
Turns a stranger into a neighbor,
and raises up what is lowly.

HADEWIJCH, ROMAN CATHOLIC

Since every lover is, in reality, the Beloved,
love erases all traces of separation.

MEHER BABA, SUFI

Walking the path of love is our highest duty
since we have taken on this body
in order to achieve love.
Live, breathe, meditate, move, sing, pray, die—in love
Spread the message of love, for love is the goal of life.
Let the whole world be circled in love.

SWAMI SIVANANDA, VEDANTA (HINDU)

Those who have all manner of knowledge,
but have little love,
can only stand at the very beginning
of the spiritual path.

MECHTHILD OF MAGDEBURG, ROMAN CATHOLIC

Learn to look with an equal eye upon all beings,
seeing the one Self in all.

FROM THE *SRIMAD BHAGAVATAM*, VEDANTA (HINDU)

One who is perfect appears to be a man but in reality is God.
He is not subject to the impermanence of the material life,
but to his great credit allows himself to consort with those who are.
Even though he is pure, he can abide those who are not.
For those who do not know Tao, he can manifest it with a glance,
thereby undoing erroneous intentions.

CHUANG TZU, TAOIST

Love makes what is bitter, sweet.
Love converts copper into gold.

JELALUDDIN RUMI, SUFI

Love implies that you are dividing yourself
between the lover and the beloved.
But if you find that place inside of you that is love,
you will no longer even love yourself.
You will just be love.

Osho, Vedanta (Hindu)

Just as a mother watches over her child,
and is willing to sacrifice herself for its protection,
so should we cherish all living beings,
encircling the world with loving kindness.

The Buddha

Never denounce anyone.
If you are willing, lend a helping hand.
If not, fold your hands and bless others,
allowing them to continue their own journey.

Swami Vivekananda, Vedanta (Hindu)

Human love sometimes fills us

and at other times leaves us empty—

like a flowering plant withering

and blooming with the seasons.

But in the deepest places

and on the highest peaks,

Love remains unchanging—ever constant.

HADEWIJCH, ROMAN CATHOLIC

You have heard it said, "An eye for an eye and a tooth for a tooth."

But I say to you, do not resist one who is evil.

But if anyone strikes you on the right cheek,

turn to him the other also;

and if anyone would sue you and take your coat,

let him have your cloak as well;

and if anyone forces you to go one mile,

go with him two miles.

Give to him who begs from you,

and do not refuse him who would borrow from you.

JESUS

A fire rages in my heart
and has made me mad with love.

MIRABAI, VEDANTA (HINDU)

To truly understand the meaning of compassion
means to understand the interdependence of all living beings.
We are all part of one another.

THOMAS MERTON, ROMAN CATHOLIC

If I speak in the tongues of men
and of angels, but have not love,
I am a noisy gong or a clanging cymbal.
And if I have prophetic powers,
and understand all mysteries and all knowledge,
and if I have all faith, so as to move mountains,
but have not love, I am nothing.
If I give away all I have,
and if I deliver my body to be burned,
but have not love, I gain nothing.
Love is patient and kind;
love is not jealous or boastful;

it is not arrogant or rude.

Love does not insist on its own way;

it is not irritable or resentful;

it does not rejoice at wrong,

but rejoices in the right.

Love bears all things,

believes all things,

hopes all things,

endures all things.

Love never ends; as for prophecies,

they will pass away;

as for tongues, they will cease;

as for knowledge,

it will pass away.

. . . So faith, hope, love abide, these three;

but the greatest of these is love.

PAUL: I CORINTHIANS, THE NEW TESTAMENT

———

If you wish to live a divine life,

have boundless love for the whole world.

Give up all hate and enmity.

Let your mind be wholly consumed by love.

BUDDHIST PRAYER

We find our own soul in those persons we love.
This is the same Supreme Soul that exists
both in ourselves and all others.

RABINDRANATH TAGORE, VEDANTA (HINDU)

Love never seeks its own will.
It is ever patient, kind and generous—
always sincere.
To seek one's own will is to fall from love.

THOMAS A' KEMPIS, ROMAN CATHOLIC

My religion is simple and has no need for temples
or philosophy, other than the philosophy of love.
No matter what a person's religious beliefs or lack of,
there is no one who is not grateful for kindness
and compassion.

TENZIN GYATSO, HIS HOLINESS THE FOURTEENTH DALAI LAMA,
TIBETAN BUDDHIST

Love is like the flame of a lamp or candle.
It cannot help but give light to others.

HAZRAT INAYAT KHAN, SUFI

All along it was Love that dragged her forward
and taught her to find her own path.
This she followed even though it took great effort,
was burdened by desires, feelings of powerlessness and unrest.
There have been many troubles and much grief.
There have been times of great faith
and times when faith was lacking.
But she is ready now for everything that comes her way.
Whether she is dead or alive,
she seeks nothing more than to be love's possession.

BEATRICE OF NAZARETH, ROMAN CATHOLIC

Love is always vulnerable and receptive.
It is sensitivity at its greatest.
But love cannot hold up where there
is self-centeredness.
Love and the personal ego are mutually exclusive.

J. KRISHNAMURTI

Practice friendliness
and your harsh feelings about others will decrease.
Practice compassion,
and your tendency to become annoyed will diminish.
Cultivate feelings of joy
and your dislike of things will grow less.
Become peaceful and balanced within yourself
and your aversion to things and people will cease.

THE BUDDHA

Love can never claim possession of anything.
Its nature is to give freedom.

RABINDRANATH TAGORE, VEDANTA (HINDU)

In truly loving others, one can more naturally
acquire the ability to let go of the world.

RAMAKRISHNA, VEDANTA (HINDU)

Love does not ask anything for itself.
Nor does it seek to protect itself
from that which is difficult.
Rather, it seeks to construct heaven
within one's heart.

WILLIAM BLAKE

Love, make me your servant.
Consume me totally and let me be your breath.

JOHN OF THE CROSS, ROMAN CATHOLIC

Lord, where there is hatred, let me sow love.

FRANCIS OF ASSISI, ROMAN CATHOLIC

If you wish to attend to me,
then take care of the sick and those in need.

THE BUDDHA

That which you do unto others, you do unto me.

JESUS

The best relationship is when
your love for someone is greater
than your need from that person.

TENZIN GYATSO, HIS HOLINESS THE FOURTEENTH DALAI LAMA,
TIBETAN BUDDHIST

With a heart absorbed in God,
one's attraction to family and friends passes away,
and compassion for them takes its place.

SRI RAMAKRISHNA, VEDANTA (HINDU)

The love a holy person has for all beings
has an effect on those beings.
If this were not the case,
the sage would not even realize he loved others.
But such a person does not need confirmation
of his love. It is simply there,
and all of humanity may rest within it.

CHUANG TZU, TAOIST

The first manifestation of love is the ability to let others
be precisely who and what they are.
Otherwise we would be looking to love
only that part of them that reflects ourselves.

THOMAS MERTON, ROMAN CATHOLIC

If we truly love God, then we naturally love others.
Loving others is the most practical way to love God.

MEHER BABA, SUFI

—∞—

True religion is the ability to devote your life to loving others.
What you do only for yourself is not religion.

SWAMI VIVEKANANDA, VEDANTA (HINDU)

—∞—

Everything we do affects the world every moment,
whether we intend it or not.
Working on our own consciousness, then,
is also the supreme creative act of love.
For everything we think and everything we do
is interconnected with the thoughts and actions
of everyone else.

RAM DASS, VEDANTA (HINDU)

ENLIGHTENMENT/AWAKENING

—⟨⟩⟨⟩⟨⟩—

Even though he is happy he has glimpses of something more.
There is a longing of the heart he cannot explain.
There is a remembering of a place just out of reach.
There is something imprinted on his soul;
something there, something eternal—
waiting for him.

KALIDASA, VEDANTA (HINDU)

—⟨⟩⟨⟩⟨⟩—

First the spark caught fire and I burst into flames.
Over and over again this happened throughout life—
until luminosity streamed from within
and surrounded me.

PIERRE TEILHARD DE CHARDIN, ROMAN CATHOLIC

I proceeded from the un-manifest
and set up my tent in the material realm.
I passed through the mineral, plant and animal kingdoms
until I reached the human heart.
There I tarried among good men until
I found the path that leads to Him.
And in finding Him, I became His slave.
Duality disappeared and I became
totally absorbed in Him.

KHWAJA ABDULLAH ANSARI, SUFI

From that day forward when the Lord
anointed me with glory, I have consumed no food
and ceased to remember earthly pleasures.

I ENOCH, JEWISH APOCHRYPHA

One who knows others becomes wise,
but one who knows himself
becomes enlightened.

THE TAO TE CHING, TAOIST

There is no greater fire than craving,
no greater crime than hatred,
no greater sadness than separation,
no worse sickness than hunger,
and no greater joy than freedom.

THE BUDDHA

Samadhi is the final transformation
that fulfills the purpose of evolution.
In this state of consciousness,
the process by which evolution unfolds
through time is understood.
This is Enlightenment.

PATANJALI, THE YOGA SUTRAS, VEDANTA (HINDU)

In the congregation of the enlightened ones
there have been many cases of mastering
the Way while working with plants and trees.
But whether working with plants or with fences or walls,
any practice that is sincere will lead to enlightenment.

DOGEN, ZEN BUDDHIST

When Samadhi is attained,
everything appears equal;
there are no more distinctions
between good and bad, this and that.

RAMAKRISHNA, VEDANTA (HINDU)

In the beginning, before I practiced Zen for many years,
I perceived mountains as mountains and waters as waters.
When I reached a deeper understanding,
I no longer saw mountains as mountains or waters as waters.
But now that I have arrived at the very essence of things,
mountains are once again mountains and waters are once again waters.

CHING-YUAN, CHAN BUDDHIST

I delight in the Holy One.
My beloved, be married in love;
Lift up your voice and give thanks to your King.
Let there be songs and music in my bridal chamber,
for under the apple tree, You have awakened me.

ELEAZAR BEN KALLIR, JEWISH

Few are they who cross over the river to the other side.

Most remain on this side, running this way and that—stranded.

But the man of wisdom crosses over.

Reaching the far shore he is beyond the reach of death.

Now he is free of darkness, free of cravings,

Rejoicing in freedom, he lets his pure light shine.

THE BUDDHA

If having reached this human form is joyous,

how much greater is the joy of knowing that

after countless incarnations,

we can look forward to the infinite?

Accepting life as it comes,

one can reach that source which lies

behind all changing phenomena.

CHUANG TZU, TAOIST

I awaken and find myself in His body.
Each part of me—my hand, my foot is Him.
Everything becomes the Godhead—indivisible.
If this seems like blasphemy,
then open your hearts and receive Him
who has opened Himself to you.

SYMEON THE NEW THEOLOGIAN, EASTERN ORTHODOX

With the sound of water falling into a stone bowl,
suddenly the dust of your mind has been washed away.

SEN-NO-RIKYU, ZEN BUDDHIST

Who am I? Who am I?
When this thought replaces all other thoughts
it becomes like a stick turning burning coals
until it is entirely burned up in the fire.
Then Self-realization dawns.

RAMANA MAHARSHI, VEDANTA (HINDU)

In the marketplace, in seclusion, I saw only God.
He has been sitting beside me through
every tribulation and good fortune.
Whether fasting or praying, praising or contemplating,
I saw only God.

I was melting like a candle in His fire,
and when I looked with God's eyes, I saw only God.
I passed away to nothingness,
vanishing to become the All-living,
and I saw only God.

BABA KUHI OF SHIRAZ, SUFI

Light exists in a person enlightened,
and it illuminates the world.
But if the light does not shine,
then there is nothing but darkness.

JESUS, *THE GOSPEL OF THOMAS*

If you fear judgment and punishment,
then why don't you seek enlightenment
all the more?
In the enlightened state,
punishment is unreality.

SRI CHINMOY, VEDANTA (HINDU)

O everlasting bliss, I have attained thee.
No longer will I be returning here.

KABIR, SUFI

Nirvana puts an end to suffering like
medicine puts an end to illness.
It is like the mountain—
free of all desire and preferences.

THE BUDDHA

Enlightenment is like the moon in water.

Moon doesn't get wet, water isn't broken.

All that is above—moon and sky—

is reflected in a single dewdrop on a blade of grass.

DOGEN ZENJI, ZEN BUDDHIST

No longer will I try to save this old pail.
The bottom has finally fallen out.
No longer will it hold water,
nor the moon reflected in it.

CHIYONO, ZEN BUDDHIST

The enlightened will shine like the zohar of the sky,
and those who make the masses righteous will shine
like the stars forever and ever.

DANIEL 12:3, THE BIBLE

Whoever knows Him in perfect knowledge,
will rest in Him who has no beginning and no end.

THE SOPHIA OF JESUS CHRIST, GNOSTIC-CHRISTIAN

Once the light came and bathed me in Truth,
I gave up all planning and plotting.
If you wish to find transcendence,
leave your little self behind and realize
that your true Self is the essence of God.
In water I saw myself as a mirage.
Becoming the ocean, I saw myself as a fleck of foam.
When I remembered, I saw that I had forgotten.
When I woke up I found that I had been asleep.

BINAVI BADAKHSHANI, SUFI

With my ignorance dispelled
I saw my former perception as confused and unclear
like sky in clouds reflected in churning water.
Now my vision is no longer clouded.
It is as clear as shining crystal.
Beyond unknowing is sun-light brilliance.
Confusion vanishes; all is perfect light.

MILAREPA, TIBETAN BUDDHIST

The day of karma has ended,
the soul is free forever.
No more birth or death.
No more I and you.
No more God and man.
Just the All—and bliss.

SWAMI VIELAMMADA, VEDANTA (HINDU)

Returning to the origin
is peace everlasting.
Destiny is eternity.
Knowing eternity
is enlightenment.

THE TAO TE CHING, TAOIST

The Lord opened my spiritual eye
and I saw the soul in the midst of my heart.
It was like an eternal and endless world.
I saw the blessed kingdom and understood.

JULIANA OF NORWICH, ROMAN CATHOLIC

As all rivers flow to the sea,
the wise return to the infinite
Light of the Supreme Being.

THE MANDAKA UPANISHAD, VEDANTA (HINDU)

Now that you've crossed the river, my friend,
where will you go?
No water, no boat, no road ahead, no traveler.
With Self forgotten, there is no within,
Not even a void to seek.

KABIR, SUFI

On that last day I was in
the presence of a totally new energy,
surrounded by a light that was so intense
that it was almost unbearable.
I felt like I was exploding,
as if I was going mad with bliss.

OSHO, VEDANTA (HINDU)

At last I see to the depths
of an ocean without water.
No obstacles anywhere.
It is all around me.

JOHO, CHAN BUDDHIST

Listen, my people: I am merging with the Elemental.

Pain and suffering are fading away.

I am returning to the Mother.

I have done everything, through many incarnations,

but now I will come and go no more.

YESHE TSOGYEL, TIBETAN BUDDHIST

The mirror of the mind is clear of all obstacles.

It illuminates the entire universe—

present even in a grain of sand.

Clarity everywhere—beyond outer and inner.

YOKA GENKAKU, ZEN BUDDHIST

When we become free of all of life's cares—

family, wealth, social position,

the darkness begins to lift,

and we find the Sea of Bliss.

RAMANA MAHARSHI, VEDANTA (HINDU)

—∿∿—

Who are you, really? Where did you come from?

Great is your ignorance.

Man is foolish. When he is a child he plays with his toys.

In his youth he is bewitched by love.

When he is old, he is bent over with cares.

The hours go by swiftly. Seasons come and go.

Finally, life runs out.

Birth leads to death and death leads to rebirth.

Where is the joy in this?

Yet the wise point to another way,

a bridge over the sea of change.

SHANKARA, VEDANTA (HINDU)

—∿∿—

The whole secret of existence is to have no fear.

Never fear what will become of you. Depend on no one.

Only the moment you reject all help are you freed.

THE BUDDHA

There is neither creation nor destruction,
neither destiny nor free will, neither path
nor achievements. This is the final truth.

RAMANA MAHARSHI, VEDANTA (HINDU)

Once upon a time there was a puppet made of salt who
had traveled a long time through dry and desert places
until one evening he came to the sea which he had
never before seen and didn't know what it was . . .
The puppet asked the sea: "Who are you?"
"I am the sea" it replied.
"But" the puppet insisted, "what is the sea?"
"I am."
"I don't understand" said the puppet made of salt.
The sea replied, "That's easy, touch me."
The salt puppet timidly touched the sea with the tip of his toes.
At that moment he realized that the sea began to make itself
perceptible,
but at the same time he noticed the tips of his toes had disappeared.
"What have you done to me?" He cried to the sea.
"You have given a little of yourself to understand me," the sea replied.
Slowly the salt puppet began to walk into the sea
with great solemnity as though he were about to perform the most
important act of his life. The further he moved along, the more he
dissolved, but at the same time he had the impression that he knew
more and more about the sea.
Again and again the puppet asked, "What is the sea?"
until the wave covered him completely.
Just before he was entirely dissolved by the sea he exclaimed:
"I exist!"

ANONYMOUS

ABOUT THE AUTHOR

Richard Hooper is a former Lutheran pastor with degrees in both theology and the philosophy of world religions. He has been a nationally syndicated radio commentator on religion and a columnist for United Press International's web forum: *www.ReligionandSpirituality.com*, and is the founder of The Sedona Institute for Comparative Theology. His website is *www.sanctuarypublications.com*.